LEAVE FROM ABSENCE

by Paul Heingarten

Published by Decatur Media
New Orleans, Louisiana
www.decaturmedia.com

ISBN: # 978-0-9972626-0-5

Acknowledgements

First and foremost, thank you to my wife Andrea, for your constant support of and belief in me and all my crazy plans and schemes. I love you!

To my parents, thanks for always being there for me and encouraging me to reach for my goals, even when they exceeded my grasp.

To great friends Tony M. Strong and Sonya Sargent. Endless thanks for your brilliant design work, the creation of this book cover, and for just being two super nice and wonderful people. I'm so glad we met. Tony is a fantastic author who's got several books on Amazon now; look for his thriller, "What Vengeance Comes" on Amazon!

To Laura Berwick, my fellow musician and writer. Thanks for your friendship, and for all your diligent efforts in helping me get this book edited and ready.

To the Bayou Writers Club: Andrea, Lisa, Dawn, Dennis, Brenda, Libby, Jill, Tony, Sonya, Clayton, Lee, and all the others. Thanks for taking the time to read this manuscript, and for giving me the critique I needed to hear rather than just the one I wanted to hear. Special thanks to Lisa Herrington for month after month helming such an amazing and important group for writers at any level of progress.

To all the people I've met and interacted with on Twitter over recent years, in no particular order: Stephen, Tara, BJ, Aja, Andy, Melissa, Kelly. Thanks for your support, encouragement, beta reading, and for showing me another side of the creative process I never even considered before.

Dedicated in loving memory of my mother Bobbie, who read the first draft of this novel and who never stopped encouraging me no matter what I tried in life.

I love you and miss you terribly, mom.

Chapter One

"Michael, GET OUT!"

The words hung in the air like the smell of rotting meat. Michael faced his father John with an incredulous look on his face. "Dad, gimme a few days."

"No, son," John retorted. "Enough already."

"Come on."

"No! You drop out of college and think nothing changes?"

Michael shrugged, and ran his hands through his hair. His dad had a point, their living arrangement depended on Michael's college enrollment.

"Dad, it wasn't working."

John shook his head, and strode past Michael in the family TV room. "You're gonna learn, son. Actions have consequences. Don't make me call the police."

"John, no!" Michael's mother interjected. "It's late, anyway. Let's cool this for a night and have him move out in the morning."

He glanced at his mother for some other sign of support. She merely returned a half-hearted shrug. "Oh don't run to me."

"Mom, please."

"No, you let me down too.

"I need more time."

"You have til morning."

"No," John corrected her. "I haven't busted my ass all these years to have my own son lie around and just soak up the benefits."

"What about my business with Jack," Michael retorted.

"Oh what, a limo service? Come on, son."

"It's gonna work, dad."

"You expect me to believe that's your ticket to wealth?"

"Dad, I can't do what you want me to do. Why can't you understand?"

"You need a good hard dose of reality, and if hitting the streets is what it takes, then so be it."

"School wasn't doing it for me, okay?"

"You won't sit here and throw your life away on my watch."

"So you're just gonna throw me away?"

"You're gonna understand some day, what I'm talking about."

Michael felt a little like he faced a firing squad. He took off for his room, and grabbed a pack. After he filled it with essentials, grabbed his laptop, and surged back into the family room. "I can't believe you'd call the cops on me. Dad, why?"

"Simple, you didn't hold up your end of the bargain, son."

He regarded them both, John with one hand on his hip, the other thrust toward the front door, Barbara slightly more reserved, her lower lip and eyes conveyed her disappointment.

His voice broke slightly as he managed to get out, "Check the news if you wanna know if I'm still alive or not." He slammed the door to the house, and headed to his car.

***

After he weaved his car down a few streets, Michael pulled over and called who he hoped had a slightly more sympathetic ear.

"Michael?"

"Hey Jack."

"What's up?"

"Whole lot."

"Like what?"

"Came into some shit at my house."

2

"Um, okay?"

"Mind if I crash at your place for a night?"

"What happened?"

"Ahh dad and mom found out I dropped out of school."

"Oh. Didn't like that huh?"

"Yeah no."

A slight pause on the other end, then Jack replied, "Tell them about the limo service?"

"Mmmm yeah didn't impress them one bit."

"What about your chauffeur's license?"

"Yeah, showed it to them and everything."

"Do I have to show them the loan papers or something?" Jack chuckled.

"Right now, I'm just the ingrate who quit school to them. That's all they care about."

"Huh. Well come on, dude. Gotcha covered for at least one night."

"Thanks, owe you big." Michael smiled as he turned the car toward Jack's apartment. He and Jack had met in little league and kept in touch through the years. They were survivors of the same high school and had each other's backs on more than one occasion.

Michael darted through the late night streets of Metairie into nearby Kenner and Jack's complex. Relieved to have a place for now, Michael hauled his bag up the stairs to Jack's apartment.

***

"Dude, that's rough," Jack said.

Michael sat on Jack's couch, sipped an Abita Amber, and explained the details that led up to being kicked out by his parents. Jack sat in his easy chair which faced Michael. As he half listened, and half mulled over advice to offer, Jack leaned back with his own beer bottle on the chair arm like a judge held a gavel.

"Yeah, well I was busting my ass in school. Really was. It just wasn't coming together. Maybe it was my major, I dunno."

"Engineering isn't exactly easy."

"No, but even before I got to the major classes, it was like they were speaking another language."

"Didn't you have some crazy course load too?"

Michael ran a hand through his hair, and took another swig of beer. "Full time plus, man. Eighteen hours for more than one semester."

"Ouch. Yeah, that would've fried my brain."

"I was holding my own for awhile, but you know my dad, always pushing me to do more, achieve more."

Jack nodded along. "Just like a salesman." Jack knew all about salespeople, as he was an IT consultant for Quicksolve, the busiest tech firm in New Orleans, thanks to their sales force. A good problem for any business, but he shook his head at the sales department's goal setting and frequent in-office pep rallies. Those people were too type A for type A people.

"If I'd just done like you, man, went summers, wrapped up a little early, and graduated ahead of time. I'd be off and running now," Michael sighed.

"It wasn't easy. I didn't sleep much and almost collapsed, remember?"

"Yeah, you were pretty bloodshot back then."

"Probably how my insomnia started."

"Hey, kudos to you, man. And now more than ever, time to make JM Limos work," Michael smiled.

"That'd be nice."

"Sure thing, the limo kings of New Orleans," Michael smiled, adding, "One day."

"Would love to stop punching a clock for these sadistic bastards."

"I'd settle for just showing my dad look, I wasn't BS'ing you after all."

"And I could quit my other ventures."

Michael shook his head, and replied, "Other ventures? Where do you find the time?"

"Dude, sometimes ya gotta put people off a little."

"I bet Ashlyn wouldn't like to hear you say that." Michael chuckled. "Where is she, anyway?"

"Working an event tonight."

Michael leaned back to stretch. Jack added, "She's gonna be here over the weekend though so, let's see what you can get before

4

then, ya know?"

Michael fetched two more beers, and plunked back on the couch. "Isn't that nice? Alright, yeah I understand."

"I'd tell you try this complex but I don't know you'd swing the rent."

"I think I can get in on the apartment behind B&G Grocery, but I have to check with the owner tomorrow on how soon."

"Cool, didn't realize they owned that place. Think they'll let an employee rent it?"

"I think so, it's been vacant for awhile. Maybe I can make 'em a deal on the rent."

"If it doesn't happen you can have another day or two, but don't push your luck, okay?" Jack warned.

"Totally, man. So when are we gonna hang out again, us, Ashlyn and Sarah?"

"Soon. Maybe a night at Ales is in order?"

"Yeah, nice. Been too long since we all hung out." Michael swigged his beer.

"I'll check with Ashlyn."

"Besides, we need to catch up with Sarah soon."

"Don't need Ales for that," Jack laughed, motioning to his laptop on the kitchen table. "Besides, I'm sure you didn't have time to catch *Stewardesses* tonight."

Michael sighed. *Stewardesses* was a TV show that had premiered a few weeks earlier, and gotten the attention of a small but growing and dedicated fan base. Michael had caught the series from the first episode, and was all over the Facebook group, chatting with people dissecting each episode as it aired. He'd also taken a liking to one of the *Stewardesses* cast, Charlotte Ducrest, a Canadian star who'd made a big impression with many viewers.

"Gotta wait til tomorrow to see it online, so don't say shit," Michael warned, chuckling a little.

"Okay, no problem. Come on, I bet Sarah's hanging around on Facebook."

***

No sign of Sarah online yet. Jack browsed through his account.

Michael pulled a chair up next to him. "No spoilers, don't click on the *Stewardesses* group alright?" Michael asked.

Jack scoffed. "Waah, waah. Look, long as you're here, let's work on a Facebook group for the limos."

Michael shrugged, "Sure thing, sounds cool."

"Winter formals and all?"

"Hey, look. She's on."

How goes it?

> Hey, some episode, huh? I thought for sure one of those Haitian rebels was going to shoot someone on the plane. And how about Monique and Tim, finally getting a little romance? Why don't I get to kiss the cute pilot? *pouts*

Michael cringed. Jack said, "Dude, how could she know, hang on."

Yeah, yeah, great stuff. Listen, got a situation over here. Michael's here and he hasn't seen the episode yet, so no more spoilers, K?

> Um... okayyy? A situation? What's going on?

"You wanna tell it, or let me?" Jack asked.

Michael tapped his shoulder. "I got this. Better get some more brews."

"Okay, but I'm not your damn bartender, alright?"

Michael plunked down in Jack's seat.

Hey Sarah, it's Michael.

Dad kicked me out.

                                    Holy shit.
                                    Why?

Told them about dropping
out, that did it.

                        They took that agreement
                                to heart, huh?

Ya think? Yeah, soon as I
told them I dropped out, it
was all over. They gave
me a few minutes to leave,
or they'd throw my ass in
jail.

                        Excessive much? Glad
                        you have a place to stay.
                        In any case, I could've set
                        you up with a friend on
                        the inside if they did bust
                        you :)

Sarah was talking about Jimmy, the father of her two kids, and also one of the more notorious meth dealers in Jefferson Parish. He was in Jefferson Parish Detention Center for at least another few months on a possession charge.

You haven't given up on
him yet?
                        Not til I collect on him.

He couldn't sell a painting
down by Jackson Square
even with all those tourists
around. Never seen him
doing much else.

                        Bastard owes me big.
Don't hold your breath.

Jack returned with more beers. "Ask her about Ales yet?"
"No, in a minute." Michael replied, to which Jack scoffed. Michael eyed Jack for a moment.

Hey Sarah, still Michael

here. When are you
working Ales again? Jack
has some hot chick he
wants to show off to us
over there.

Tomorrow through and
Saturday, the usual.
Come on by. Hot chick?
Do tell, Jack.

Jack returned Michael's Cheshire Cat grin with a frown.
"Yeah, keep it up and you'll be out of two homes in one night."

Oh, it's just Ashlyn.

Oh cool, been missing her!

Jack popped Michael on the back of his head.
"OWW!"
"Don't be trashin my woman!" Jack chuckled.
"Alright, okay, damn." Michael glanced at Jack over his
shoulder.

So, how goes life otherwise?

Non-stop chaos. My kids'
school is giving me hell
about having updated
vaccination records when
I KNOW I mailed them to
the nurse last year. Did
they burn the files over
summer vacation?

How else would they hide
how poorly run the public
education system is?

Ha ha! Now I've got to
squeeze in a trip to the
doctor's office this week
to get the school
administrators off my ass.

Michael glanced at Jack. He leaned back in a chair, his feet propped on one side of the computer desk.

Sarah, we're into the 21st century now. Can't your doctor's office just scan and email the records over and save everyone some trouble?

It would make sense to just do that, wouldn't it? Well, according to school board requirements they need an original hard copy of the records. I can't even scan a copy and email it to them. Fucking bureaucrats. I'll also be working a double at the bar next weekend, and, oh yes, my lovely radio job still awaits me.

Wow, Sarah you don't just have a full plate. You've got a platter.

Don't I know it. Speaking of platter, I got an email from my sister Kelly in New York. She's having a ball up there, busting her ass in school at the Culinary Institute of America!

Wait... Culinary Institute of America. The CIA??? LOL

Mmm yeah, guess if you like.

What, they cook for people and then kill them?

Wellll let's hope not.

Hah! Kelly was always was into cooking, I

9

remember. That's
awesome!

Ikr? Short of getting
whisked away by Dave
Grohl and becoming his
live in lover, my dreams
lie with big sis getting her
own restaurant and
setting me up pretty. So,
you guys want to come by
the bar tomorrow, so I
can see Jack's hottie? I
can probably get you a
few free drinks.

You had me at free drinks!

Well I need to get some
sleep, I'm sure you do
too, fanboy.

Yeah true, gonna sign off
for now. I'll give you all
the gory details you want
when we see you at Ales.
Nite!

Good night you two! It'll
be nice to see y'all again!

Michael logged off, and shut down Jack's computer as they
prepared to turn in for the night. He thought about how both Sarah
and Jack always had a lot going on. Jack worked at a steady nine-
to-five job, pulled in a good salary, and he busted his ass on those
home business ideas. Sarah, on top of her two jobs, had her two
sons.

His thoughts lingered on Sarah. He wondered if she ever
thought about that night, years ago. She hadn't spoken of it since.
Neither had Michael himself, for that matter. She was too busy
trying to hold her life together, he guessed. And he was just trying
to get to point B while being stuck on point A forever. He had to
wonder, *do enough wrong turns in life finally end up equaling a
right one?*

Chapter Two

B&G Grocery was a Metairie institution. It was a small, family-owned grocery store that survived the various national chains that had moved into the surrounding area over the years. B&G's prices weren't the cheapest, but the owners prided themselves on a level of customer service that the big stores never offered.

Ray, the assistant manager, looked at his watch as Michael clocked in five minutes late, and shook his head. "Nice of you to join us, Michael." He handed him the cash register till for the day. Michael mouthed a quick "Sorry" as he went to his check out aisle.

Mornings at B&G tended to be full of quick shoppers. Nine-to-fiver's who didn't have time to fix breakfast at home, and just wanted a quick something on their way to work; housewives who needed a beverage on their way to or from their morning exercise routine; the occasional retiree who enjoyed some hot, fresh bread from the B&G bakery. B&G proudly stocked all the New Orleans staples like Community Coffee, various types of red kidney beans, Leidenheimer French bread, NOLA Brewery beer, and more.

Michael settled into his routine at the cash register. After several months at the job, it became mindless. Groceries scanned, vegetables weighed, orders bagged, money collected, etc. A lot of the time, he never even looked directly at the people in his checkout line. When he did, most of them were distracted by their phones, or maybe a magazine they grabbed in the checkout.

It wasn't always mundane. He found ways to amuse himself. He chuckled to himself over the people who came through his line with boxes of junk food and one little bottle of Vitamin Water, like that magically offset the eight million calories from the rest of their haul.

Michael noticed Ray nearby as he finished with a customer. "Hey, uh, is Ms. Rose here yet?"

Ray glanced around. "No, she'll be in around 10:30 or so. Need something?"

"Yeah, but it's about that apartment in the back."

Ray nodded. "Come up front around lunchtime, she should be around then."

As the day progressed, customers bought more real groceries. They purchased carts full of food for large meals. Sometimes, Michael thought about the items people bought, and what that said about them. When he shopped, he bought snacks and beer.

In Michael's mind, people who bought more items than him were doing more with themselves than he was. A person who cooked a meal was self-sufficient, probably employed, maybe someone with a family. *Well maybe once the limo business takes off I'll be right in there with them, hassling some kid cashier about not moving fast enough,* he mused.

***

As he tended to his slow but steady stream of customers, Michael's mind sometimes wandered into daydreams, when thoughts about the groceries people bought simply weren't enough. To everyone else, he seemed to be alert and on the job, even if the look in his eyes was somewhat distracted. Ever since *Stewardesses*, though, his dream moments felt like he was in an episode of the series. In his mind, he was on a passenger jet circa 1960. It was an overseas flight, and he sat in the first class cabin,

12

of course. He looked at a *Life Magazine* when he heard a familiar voice, *"Would you like something to drink?"*

Michael glanced up, and saw Charlotte as her character Monique. He smiled at her and said, "I'd love a whiskey sour, Monique." Monique left after she offered a smile and nod to him. Michael imagined he was a salesman, on a trip to England to get a multinational contract secured for his company. Some huge business deal that meant a lot of recognition, and a nice sum of money for him.

Monique handed him his drink and asked, "So, what brings you to Jolly Old England?"

Michael smiled, and took a sip. "I'm on a mission to secure a new contract for my company."

"Oh my, it sounds very important."

"Sure thing."

"How long will you be staying?"

"It depends. I'm hoping to wrap this up inside of a week, but I guess that depends on how cooperative the other guys are."

Monique laughed, "Yes, indeed. It does take two."

He took another sip of his drink, and regarded Monique more carefully. "You know, I'm not going to be working the whole time I'm there."

Monique arched an eyebrow.

"I hear England has many interesting sights to see in general."

"Mais oui, certainement! Oh, forgive me. I sometimes slip into French when I get excited."

"It's fine, really."

"Of course, there are things to see. Perhaps you could use a tour guide?"

Michael nodded slowly. "Well only if she's as fetching as you are."

Monique blushed, and giggled softly. "I suppose we should make plans to get together then."

They smiled at each other, as they enjoyed the moment. Just as Michael took a sip of his drink, the cabin of the plane shook violently. Caught off guard, Monique thrust her arms out, and braced herself.

Michael's drink was jostled, and spilled a little onto his seat

13

and pants. Ever the conscientious stewardess, Monique glanced down commenting, "Oh dear, let me get something to clean that up." She glanced up to see Leigh, the head stewardess and purser on the flight, toward the front of the plane.

Leigh, another stewardess, made her way down the aisle fast. As she passed them, she commented to Monique, "Better batten down the hatches, rough cross winds."

Monique nodded in reply, and then turned to Michael. Her hair swirled around her shoulders, almost as if it were part of some elaborate dance move. Smiling politely, she said, "I'm so sorry. I'll have to attend to that spill in just a moment, once this turbulence passes."

"That's quite alright, don't want you in harm's way on my account."

Winking, she replied, "And thank you for understanding."

At that moment, the plane lurched forward and to the side considerably. Monique's grasp on the chair wasn't strong enough, and she fell toward Michael. He reached instinctively to catch her as she fell.

As she landed in his arms, Monique let out a small cry. She looked up to find herself locked into a gaze with Michael. "Oh mon Dieu, you caught me! Thank you."

"Easy, you're fine."

"I hope I can repay you!"

Michael searched Monique's eyes. He hadn't dreamed how they would look from this close up. He felt momentarily dazed by her beauty. He was holding her in his arms, after all. He reached for something clever to say. "I know, how about a date once we get to England?"

She eyed him with a mixture of surprise and intrigue.

Michael added, "You can show me some of the sights."

"Oh, I imagine such an act of gallantry would warrant a nice meal together. How much do your oranges cost?"

Michael was confused. "Oranges? What are you talking about?"

Monique spoke again, but her voice had changed. "Oranges, how much are they? The price sign isn't up there anymore."

He was jarred out of his pleasant daydream with Monique, and

14

found himself under the gaze of a middle aged, heavyset woman in curlers. He blinked down at a laminated sheet of produce prices, and rattled off the listed price, "$2.99 a pound." The woman nodded, and walked off.

It seemed so real when he daydreamed like this. But before long, his bubble burst, and he dropped abruptly back into his reality that he was a cashier. *Maybe one day, something bigger will come,* he thought.

***

Michael stopped for lunch around 1pm. He sat in the break room, ate his sandwich from the B&G Deli, and sipped his Coke. Coins jingled in the soft drink machine, and Michael turned to Ms. Rose, who was getting a drink.

"Ms. Rose, hi, can I talk with you for a minute?"

She grabbed her drink, and opened it carefully, then faced him. "Make it quick," she said, her slurp of soft drink punctuating her sentence.

He turned in his seat. "I'm looking for a place to live, and I know y'all have that apartment in the back here. Any chance I can rent that out?"

Ms. Rose gently brushed back a lock of permed blonde hair, and adjusted her glasses. "No can do. Just got a tenant, and I don't think there's room for two."

"Oh, I didn't know."

"Yeah. Was that it?"

"You have any other places? I need something quick."

She sipped her drink, and shrugged. "We have two others, but things are full up at the moment. Sorry."

"Thanks, Ms. Rose. Have a nice--" The door slam finished Michael's sentence for him. He pounded his fist on the table. Great. So much for that. Something had to turn up soon.

After he finished lunch, he took his smart phone out, and logged into Twitter. As "@Tim707", Michael followed a number of other accounts people created for characters on *Stewardesses* like Monique.

@Tim707: Attention, passengers. Your friendly

#Stewardesses airline and crew will be departing next Wednesday at 8pm, 7pm Central #StayTuned

Another account, "@FlirtyMonique" replied to Michael's tweet a few moments later.

@FlirtyMonique: @Tim707 yes, captain. And I am most looking forward to spending more time with you on the ground as well X O.
@Tim707: @FlirtyMonique and hello to you! I hope we have a dinner date as usual. And maybe more later? ;)
@FlirtyMonique: @Tim707 Mais oui! Next time we fly to Paris I think a drive to the country is in order, and more... fun!

Michael snickered. This kind of interaction was commonplace amongst the *Stewardesses* fans on Twitter. The interactions often had little to do with the show itself, other than people who pretended to be characters, and either just chatted, or acted out longer scenes via Twitter. He sometimes wondered about the people behind these accounts. He rarely if ever saw pictures of anyone, and who knew if what these people posted were their actual pictures anyway.

The username @FlirtyMonique wasn't very familiar, but it was one of his followers. The number of people with accounts for *Stewardesses* grew rapidly in recent weeks, as fans took to Twitter, and tweeted while the episodes aired. Michael preferred to focus his full attention on the show while it was on.

Michael had enough time left on his break, so he rattled off another reply.

@Tim707: @FlirtyMonique you and I having fun, Monique. Like there's any other outcome? ;)

Several people, including Michael, had periodically tweeted using the #SaveStewardesses hash tag as a sort of unofficial petition among fans on Twitter. While no one knew for sure if network executives with power over the show's contract followed the tags, fan tweets, or even looked at Twitter at all, it meant die-hards of the series had a feeling of hope at least they did something for their show.

A call came in just then from Jack.

"Yo, what's the word?" Michael asked.

"Okay, we have an appointment next week with an insurance company."

"Awesome. Hey man, what's your rent?"

"$700 a month, why?"

"Well that B&G Apartment isn't happening. It's taken."

"Sucks dude. Yeah $700 a month, two year lease."

"A little high for me right now. And I don't guess you'd care for a roomie."

"Yeah, living with you long term might drive me nuts."

"See, thought you already were."

"Piss off. How about cars?"

"I saw a few online, I'll make a list, and show you tonight."

"Tomorrow. Ales time tonight."

"Oh you know it."

"Look, take a look online or something. Bound to be a few places for rent around."

"Yeah. Sorry, will try not to linger too long."

"Thanks. Alright, see ya tonight!"

"Yep."

Michael placed his phone in sleep mode, discarded his trash, and headed back to his register to finish his shift. As he walked, he mulled over his situation a bit more. *Hey universe, throw me a bone here. So I dropped out of school, and I'm listless. Can't you toss something good my way for once?*

Back in his work routine, his mind drifted to his parents. *They just don't get it*, he thought. *I'm not Dad. I'm never gonna fit into his perfect little idea of what a professional clock punching guy is, at least not working for someone else.* He tried to stop the thoughts about that, and just powered through the rest of his work day. It only frustrated him more when it felt like other people tried to guide his life, no matter how aimless he felt on his own a lot of the time.

He knew he had to come up with something quick. Jack had helped a lot for now, but he wasn't sure when that would run out.

Chapter Three

Sarah's Thursday morning began as usual when her alarm shattered the morning stillness at 6:00 a.m. Her left hand hit the snooze button. She repeated this motion so often, her movements were a matter of muscle memory.

Several minutes later, she sat up in bed, and shut off her alarm clock. She yawned, and ran her fingers through her hair. *Did I not just get to sleep like five minutes ago,* she thought. *Got to get the kids off to school, and head to the radio station. Oh yeah, can't forget, I need to find time to call the doctor about the immunization. Fuck Peter.*

Her slender frame of around five feet had seen plenty of action in her 22 years, from her marathon weekend shifts bartending at Ales, the radio station salespeople she chased down for her other job, and most of all everything and anything that kept her two boys in line. She slipped on a robe over her T-shirt and pajama bottoms, and walked to her kids' room.

Alex and Taylor's room was a short walk down the hallway. When she opened the door, she saw the boys groggily moved around. "Morning, my babies!" she announced warmly.

"Morning, Mom" they said in unison.

"Okay, let's get moving. Breakfast first, then bathroom and change clothes."

The boys filed out of the room, and into the kitchen. Taylor walked in front of Alex and, to mess with his younger brother, he stopped short a few times, letting Alex bump into him. With this, Alex shoved Taylor forward. After several pushes, Alex cried out, "Mom!"

"Hey, you two... cut that out. We've got less than forty-five minutes to be out that door, and on the way to school. No messing around."

Alex added a "yeah," looking at Taylor. Taylor responded by punching him on the arm.

Sarah had been putting the cereal, milk and bowls on the table. She looked at them sternly, then raised her voice, and retorted sharply, "Look, if you keep that up, you're both going to be in it deep. You got me?"

Sarah knew how to drop the hammer on her boys when it came to discipline. She was thankful her mom had been tough on her. It helped understand how to be stern with her children. Of course, it would've been nicer had Jimmy liked being a family man, and stayed around with them more than slinging meth. Loser.

The boys quietly ate their cereal as Sarah sipped her coffee. *Alright,* she thought to herself. *One situation for the day handled. Now if I can just handle the children I work with, I'll really have accomplished something.*

***

After Sarah dropped her kids off at school, she still had several hours before she had to be at the radio station. It was one of the few times she was happy not to work forty hours a week.

This was the busiest part of her week: days at the station, nights at Ales. She was relieved she had a small pocket of free time in the morning, for anything she hadn't already caught up on the rest of the week.

Sarah sat at the kitchen table, and grabbed the stack of bills stashed in her checkbook. She felt an odd satisfaction paying bills.

19

While she hated the idea of her hard earned money being spent, she also felt a sense of pride in paying her own expenses. Every check she wrote, every envelope she addressed, every stamp she attached reminded her that what she had here was hers. While she did sometimes miss an intimate connection with a guy that shared her life and financial burden, she also never wanted the role of someone's live in maid or lover. She already had that with Jimmy.

They met in high school after Sarah and Jack broke up. Despite the misgivings expressed by her mom, sister, Michael, and several others, Sarah refused to listen to anything other than her own belief she was doing the right thing. Life taught her a hard lesson when her so called love ran up some bills, and got prison time, which left her to fend for herself. She made it through that ordeal, and was determined she made her own way in the world now, and she'd never been as foolish about men ever since.

Her need for control probably came when her own family imploded after her parents' divorce when she was young. She watched her mom, who took odd jobs, and scraped by for the money that kept Sarah and Kelly fed and clothed.

Sarah's work ethic that you busted your ass, and never complained about little things people with money griped about came from all those times she watched what her mother did, and went through over the years. "Working and paying bills beats the hell out of starving to death," she often quipped to coworkers at Ales when they made their trivial problems so earth shattering.

Phone bill, cable, Internet bill, electricity, gas, doctor for the boys... she took care of them one at a time. She saved the credit card bill for last, since she never knew how much she'd racked up. Lately, she'd been using it for groceries, and things for the boys, nothing frivolous--she'd use it when she was running short, and needed some necessities before payday.

Her heart sank when she realized she wouldn't have enough for the minimum credit card payment. It wasn't the first time. Her mind began to race over things she could cut back on. Did they need that set of clothes she bought last month? Could she have hitched a ride to Ales here and there, and saved some gas money? The puzzle rearranged itself in her head. Pieces of her life that had to fit a certain way, no room to be budged.

She grabbed her pack of cigarettes, and lit one. A few quick drags while she stared at her pile of bills through the dim haze. She reassured herself, "You've been making it on your own so far, you can keep this up."

She leaned back in her chair, and considered her options. Her mother? Maybe. She knew Mom still tried to make her own ends meet though. Sarah disliked like the idea of being a burden, even on her own mother. To Sarah, that meant failure. She was determined to work this out by herself, somehow.

Sighing, she crushed her cigarette in the ashtray, and grabbed her stack of bills. As she began to sob, she thought, *Happiness isn't so much the issue right now as doing something to earn more money. I love my boys, and the life we have, but I can't be worrying about how I'm going to pay for it every damn month. Shouldn't need a damn man to have enough money. But it's more than that. I'm alone. If I could just find a guy who will BE there for me and the boys. There's only been assholes like Jimmy, and well... there's Michael. He can be a prick sometimes, but he had come through for me before. And there was that time...*

Sarah glanced up at the wall clock, and realized she had twenty minutes to get to the radio station. She caught her breath, wiped away her tears, and grabbed her purse and the pile of checks, ready to mail.

She hadn't figured it all out yet, but she knew she had to. What other choice did she have?

***

Sarah arrived at the WZEB-FM office, called the pediatrician on her mobile phone, and arranged to pick up a copy of her kids' immunization papers at lunch. Now, she just needed a quick break to get it all handled in time. She only needed Peter's cooperation. She already had to deal with two kids today, and Peter often acted just as childish in his own way.

Sarah walked to her desk. Her cubicle was outside of Peter's office, and he saw her from his desk with a little effort. "Morning, Sarah," he exclaimed.

"Morning, Peter!" she called back as she tossed her purse under her desk, and glanced at her phone message light.

Peter got up, and walked over to her. He was heavy, with a beer gut from way too many radio station live broadcasts, and the alcohol fueled evenings that always followed. Sarah sometimes looked at him, and imagined him back in college, a bloated loud-mouthed jock, for whom frat parties and skirt chasing were as much a part of the curriculum as English class. In the year or so she'd worked with Peter, he'd started toning it down a little, but he still rattled off some choice inappropriate remarks here and there. Even more when he wasn't sober.

His scraggly brown hair and beard could have made him a finalist in a Zach Galifianakis lookalike contest. But in spite of his personality and somewhat scruffy appearance, his sales record had boosted him up to a sales manager position, and kept him there for years. He was rough around the edges with his subordinates, but he knew how to get the job done.

Peter carried a file folder several inches thick. "Hey, Sarah... Need you to do me a favor. One of our sales reps quit last week, and I need you to sort through these account claim forms. You know how competitive salespeople are, jumping on fresh meat as soon as they see it. Anyway, I need you to have this done by lunch today. Also, don't forget about the monthly sales report for corporate."

"Who quit?"

"Bill."

"Wow, wasn't he number one here?"

"Yeah. Smooth talking bastard took a Local Sales Manager gig across town. Probably trashing the station soon as he hit the elevator."

Sarah chuckled softly. Bill and Peter's friendship went back several years, through their respective radio sales careers. Peter didn't put up with a lot from his subordinates, but if they were proven salespeople who time and again made their quotas, they were allowed some leeway. Bill fit that description to a T. He was known as the car dealer king in the New Orleans market, mostly because of the high octane frantically voiced commercials that he created with his own voice. Bill was also notorious in that he showed up late to sales meetings, and sneaked account information off of his colleagues' desks. He had a way of talking at, rather than with Sarah that irked her. She made a point to put any work he requested at the bottom of her to do pile, since he never gave her much consideration, either.

He wasn't someone Sarah missed, and, aside from the lost sales, neither would the station.

She took the folder from Peter, and glanced down at the file. "This AND the monthly report for today? I need a little time at lunch to run an errand." She looked back at Peter, her eyes pleaded. *Half an hour, Peter. Come on.*

Peter returned her inquisitive glance with a furrowed brow. "This has got to be sent to corporate before noon, and I need these account assignments done, so salespeople can start calling clients. You know, the reason we're here?"

"Peter, it's important."

"I need this ASAP, Sarah. Come on, help me out."

She sighed, and glanced back at the folder. "All right, I'll see what I can do."

Peter walked away from her desk. She thought, *How the hell am I going to pick these records up now? I'm screwed if I can't take care of that. And now more shit from sales. Peter can be such a pain in the ass.*

Sarah looked through the list of claim forms, and her mind began to wander. *There are people in this world that don't have to put up with this shit, She thought. Like those girls from Stewardesses. Monique, Leigh, Anne, Julie... They don't have their bosses dumping crap on them with no notice, or concern for the rest of their workload. They have their own issues, I'm sure, but they're traveling around the world. I would take some grief to see a new country every 3-5 days.*

And, along with their exotic travel came romance. Monique and Tim had been steadily building a relationship, away from the watchful eyes of their superiors, who would fire them for being together. Leigh was always finding herself into one jam or another, but still managed to snag a guy here and there, if only for a one night stand. And then, there were the sisters, Anne and Julie. Julie was new to the crew, but she still had her bit of romance. Anne was wrapped up in some espionage subplot, and had made a love connection with a Croatian diplomat.

Sarah compared her own love life to the *Stewardesses* girls.

Well, there was her teen pregnancy. Her mom had flipped, but soon regrouped, and helped Sarah get established. Jimmy had stuck around, at first. He seemed to be into painting, and tried to make a go of it. But diapers and screaming babies at all hours of the night just weren't his thing. He halfway helped at first, but then he stayed out later and later at night. He pretty much became another child she had to wrangle.

She did do a bit of moving on herself later, and she had a few flings, but nothing really took for her. The fact she was pretty hardheaded herself never helped. But to Sarah, her tough attitude was about survival and defense, not that she played hard to get. Positive examples of men in her life were in short supply. Not even her own father -- he'd left her mom when she and Kelly were still in grade school. She'd been raked over the coals enough by romance to know that while being single and alone was hard, being in a toxic relationship was far worse.

As she paged through the rough draft sales reports, full of Peter's handwritten notes on them, her phone rang. Glancing at the caller id, she saw it was Vanessa, the station promotions director. She picked up the handset. "What's up girl? Got any good swag for me?"

Vanessa laughed, "Oh what? That's how it is now?"

"Huh?"

"I hook you up with movie passes, t shirts, food for your kiddos, and now that's all I'm good for?"

"Oh you're my girl, you know that."

"Yeah yeah. So what's with these live broadcasts? I don't have locations and times, as usual."

"Typical. Um, I don't know offhand, but I'll try to corner the guilty parties this afternoon. Who is it?"

Paper rustled on the other end for a few seconds, then Vanessa spoke, "Looks like Ted once again."

Sarah grasped her forehead. "Okay, I'll jump on his ass."

"Careful, he might like that," Vanessa giggled.

"Ha! I'd rock that man's world and send him into traction! So when are we going out to lunch again?"

"This week is kind of crazy, maybe next?"

"Sounds good. Let me go. I need to work on sales numbers for Mr. Wonderful over here."

"Oh shit. Peter. Say no more."

"Talk soon! Later!"

Vanessa hung up. Sarah smiled. In the brief time she had gotten to know Vanessa at WZEB-FM, she had proven to be a great friend. Vanessa appreciated people like Sarah, and she recognized while Sarah's job was pretty important to the sales staff, Sarah never made a decent salary. Vanessa tried to send extra freebies Sarah's way whenever possible. To Vanessa, it was the least she could have done. Sarah enjoyed her company, and their lunches together had become a regular activity.

Moments later her phone rang again. She was full-on multitasking, eyes on the sales reports. "Yeah Vanessa, forget something?"

"Ms. Sarah Miller?"

The shrill voice of the principal from her boys' school jolted her mind away from the reports. A few slipped from her hands onto her desk.

"Speaking."

"Good morning, this is Principal Olsen. Your boys are in a bit of trouble at the moment."

The rest of the forms fell to Sarah's desk as she rubbed her forehead. "What did they do?"

"They thought it would be funny to hide in the girls' restroom. Ms. Miller, they will be in detention after school. Just wanted you to know."

Deep sigh. "Yes, of course."

"As you know, this is the second incident for them this month."

"Yes, I'm aware. I've been trying to work on their behavior."

"I understand, but this can't continue."

"Of course. Thank you, Principal Olsen."

"Room 113 after school."

"I'll get them when they're ready."

She shook her head a moment to switch gears, then powered through her work again. It was Thursday, and she had a two day stretch at the bar at Ales soon. And to top it off, she had two little boys to put in their place yet again.

As she flipped through the pages of sales data, she clung to the lingering hope that somewhere, somehow, she was going to find a better way to have the life she wanted.

Chapter Four

Jack sat in his cubicle. His computer was logged in, and he had the incident reporting software open and ready. He stretched his arms out over his head, and reached out to touch the picture of a limousine posted on his cubicle wall as he muttered, "Make it happen." He was stocky from spending a lot of time browsing the internet at home, and not too much time at the gym.

It was Friday morning. His office phone rang. He quickly put on his headset, and clicked the line button. "Tech support, how may I assist you?"

"Yes... uh... hello? I'm trying to add some extra luggage to my flight reservation, and my account won't let me."

"Not a problem, name and username?"

"Gina Reynolds, and my username is TennisOne63."

"Okay, Ms. Reynolds, I'll have a look. Please hold."

After he checked a few things Jack returned to the call. "Ms. Reynolds, a system glitch was hanging the baggage entry portion of our site. I had our system administrator clear this up. Give it about five minutes, and try again."

"Wonderful."

"Thanks for traveling through us!"

"Thank you as well," she said, and hung up.

Jack logged the call with his incident tracking software. This was his career, for now. Since college, he had worked for almost a year and a half at Quicksolve. He had a good rapport with his boss, got along with his co-workers for the most part, he had zero complaints from the customers he helped. It was a cozy existence for him, and for many of his co-workers it was the perfect career.

Jack's day job was almost comfortable enough to stop his thoughts about other options.

Aside from some internet startup opportunities he looked at, JM Limos was his best hope for financial freedom.

Whenever he slipped too far into the comfort zone of just working day to day, week to week, he looked at a picture he kept on the bulletin board beside his desk. It was a photo of his father when he worked at the 7UP bottling plant in town. His dad was a foreman, and did fairly well. He put in a good 15 years at the company, until the bottling plant was closed due to cutbacks and downsizing.

Jack's phone rang again. Glancing at the ID, he saw it was Ashlyn.

Tapping the line button, he said, "Hello, gorgeous."

"Hey stud."

"How are you?"

"I'm good, sweetheart. Just seeing how your day is going."

"Putting out fires, 'saving the world.'"

"Keeping our travelers safe from a reservation apocalypse?"

"Right? Also looked into another business opportunity."

"What is it?"

"Internet wholesaling. You get a website, and order stuff at wholesale. I'm selling sports stuff: jerseys, team mini helmets, mugs, things like that."

"I see. Think it'll work?"

"Maybe. Worth a try."

"This is on top of your limo idea?"

"Can't be too sure."

"Ahh right. Remember, we're having dinner with my friends Julie and Karine on Saturday."

"This Saturday?" Jack winced as he checked his planner.

"That's right. You promised you'd make time, since we've already canceled twice because of those business seminars."

"Oh yeah, here it is. Alright. I'll make it this time, I promise."

"Mmmhm."

Ashlyn was more patient than most women would be. She let Jack take the time for his various meetings, but the hunt ate away at their time together, and started to weigh on their relationship.

Jack tried to lighten the mood. "Did you give that *Stewardesses* show a watch?"

"I did. It looks okay."

"Just okay?"

"Don't know that it's for me. Too much like a soap opera. I'm stuck on reality shows, I suppose." She giggled at her last statement.

"Like *Insane Housewives*, or whoever else is hot this week?"

"Hey, it's fun."

"Fun waiting for them to fight over nothing?"

"I don't get as bogged down in the details as you, Mr. Jet Setter."

Jack laughed. "Hey, how about we hang with Michael and Sarah again. They're missing us."

Ashlyn measured her words. "Michael... and Sarah?"

"Ya know, like we used to til a month or two ago?"

"Um... has she been calling you?"

"No, no! Maybe a chat here or there online, with Michael around. Ya know, TV stuff, general BS."

"Ah. Hey, how about we get take out tonight, and have an evening in?"

"Yes! I'll regale you with more of my entrepreneurial misadventures."

"Oh baby, please." Ashlyn cooed. "Better make it worth my while."

"Don't I always?"

"A foot massage at least!"

"You got it, heart."

"I should let you get back to work. Talk to you this evening, love you!"

"Love you too!" said Jack as he hung up. Ashlyn sure had that fun quality about her. She reminded him a bit of Sarah, and how they were when he dated Sarah. He only hoped that little fact never slipped out to Ashlyn.

Chapter Five

Jack and Ashlyn sat on her couch and enjoyed some wine as they went over each other's work day.

"So this guy says our stock trading application is broken, and after a little troubleshooting, he says his laptop just might have a virus. Might!"

Ashlyn sipped her wine and remarked, "And that couldn't have anything to do with it."

Jack shrugged. "Right? Most aren't that bad. Now and then one's a real ass, spreading misery."

Ashlyn laughed, "Some people aren't into computers in general. Then again, that's job security for you, right?"

"Yep."

Ashlyn got up. "Care for a refill? We just killed that last one, but I have chardonnay. Marimar Estate, 2010 vintage?"

Jack smiled, "Oooh baby, I love when you talk vintage." He'd met her at a wine tasting class offered by a local wine store. They hit it off just about immediately. Soon after a few weeks of dates, they took a trip to California where Ashlyn wowed Jack with her in-depth knowledge of Sonoma County. Now they were just about inseparable.

As she filled the glasses, she eyed the food cartons Jack had set on the kitchen table when he first arrived. "Food smells great!" She said, as she returned with two fresh glasses, handing him one. Jack asked, "How's accounting life?"

Sipping her wine, a smile forming, she replied, "Well for starters, I'll be going for training again soon."

"Didn't you just get back from your last one?"

She nodded. "I know. Well they won't be sending me to wine country this time. More like Dallas."

"I'm sure you'll have fun. When is it?"

"About three weeks. They're finalizing the course arrangements."

Jack studied the golden hue in his glass for a moment.

"Oh!" Ashlyn sat up quickly, "This was so great. I figured out some account discrepancies they'd been trying to chase down for our rental car company. It had been a pain in their ass for a while, but I was able to clear up their books!"

"Hey!" Jack said as he raised his glass.

Ashlyn smiled. "Yeah, got a lot of kudos on that one."

Jack said, "My baby, accounting badass!" They clinked glasses.

Jack said, "Maybe you can watch *Stewardesses* with me next week. I can tell you more about the show, and maybe by then I won't still have my guest."

"Guest?"

"Yeah, Michael. Kicked out of his house."

"Kicked out?"

"Long story."

"Well that's nice of you, putting him up. You're not gonna do that for long though, right?"

"Don't think so. He's working on it. He's the 'M' of the JM Limos."

"Oh of course." Ashlyn nodded.

"And an even a bigger fan of *Stewardesses* than me."

Ashlyn laughed. "You guys act like you've never seen a stewardess before. Should I dress up as one for Halloween?"

"That'd be pretty damn hot. But yeah, Michael and Sarah

watch it with me, and we usually end up chatting on Facebook about it later."

"So what's the big deal with y'all and this show? Why is it so important to watch it?"

"It's about the 1960s, and a group of people living the life: fine dining, sex, intrigue. Me? I'm just a poor sap punching a clock, working for someone else all day."

Ashlyn's eyes narrowed in a dark, sultry gaze, and she leaned close. "You are having sex, even if you aren't going global." She kissed him.

Jack smiled in the kiss and replied, "I know. But this is escapism."

"As opposed to what I'm watching?"

"The made up reality TV?"

"Hey, it's fun, and easy to get into."

"Yeah, but things like some dopey bachelor and his twenty or so network-approved dates? *Stewardesses* is about storylines."

She slapped his leg. "Leave my reality shows alone."

Jack grinned.

Ashlyn wrinkled her nose. "How many episodes aired already?"

"Three as of this week."

"And you're already hooked?"

"It's a great show!"

"Okay, I did see a bit of last week's."

"Great. Your chance to see it is slipping away anyway."

"Why?"

"According to Michael, they may not have another season after this one."

"Not much chance for them?"

Jack shrugged. "Ratings and fan response aren't great. Anyhow, we're overdue for a TV watching date night."

"Fair enough. Now, let's get some food!" Ashlyn stood up from the sofa, and walked toward the kitchen table. Jack followed her, and turned to reach for the food cartons. The food had cooled slightly, so he grabbed two plates. She transferred the food to them, and proceeded to warm them in the microwave as he sat at the kitchen table, and watched her.

After watching the food heating for a moment, she remarked, "Suppose I won't hear the end of it until I watch this *Stewardesses* series with you."

"Hey, it'll be fun. And something else we can talk about."

"Oh we're doing pretty well so far. So, I called my friends about next Saturday, and they're both in. I figure we'll meet them for dinner around 7pm, then drinks after."

The microwave beeped. Jack took the trout dish from the microwave, then gingerly transferred the meal to the plates with a spatula. "So how do you know these people?"

"Oh, some sorority sisters I kept in touch with after college. You'll like them. I told them about us dating, and they want to meet you."

Jack cringed a bit. "That might be the night of this house flipping seminar."

Ashlyn took a sip of her wine, and pondered for a moment. "You know, I like that you're so driven to find something for yourself, I do. But now and then, a girl likes to have her boyfriend out with her."

Jack shifted as he laid the spatula down.

"Can't you blow this one off? It's a night, Jack."

"I had to be on a waiting li-"

"Come on, baby. There'll be another. I need some of your time too."

He grabbed the two plates of food, and walked around the counter to the table. He placed one plate in front of Ashlyn. "Bon appétit, hope you enjoy. I slaved over a hot microwave for three minutes for you."

Ashlyn smirked. "Uh huh, you mean my microwave." She stood up from her seat, and leaned forward. Jack smiled, and met her with a kiss standing over the table.

They sat back down, and began eating. The trout had a wonderful taste of herbs, and the soft crunchiness of the pecans made a great texture. A healthy serving of roasted corn grits and green beans complimented the fish. Jack finished a bite of food with a sip of wine and said, "Wow, that's great stuff. Gotta love Zea's." Ashlyn nodded in agreement.

Jack continued, "So I meet your friends this Saturday. When

can we meet up with Michael and Sarah?"

"Maybe tomorrow night?"

"Okay, sounds great! Ya know, Sarah and I actually dated a few times." As he heard himself say that he clenched. *It's not a thing,* he repeated to himself.

Ashlyn blinked for a moment. Her jaw tightened a bit, but she was able to manage an, "Oh really?"

"Yeah, we did."

"You never told me before."

Jack worked on an earnest smile. "It was a long time ago... high school. And not very long term."

"But you hang out with your ex still?"

"Ex from high school. I was her date for some school dances, and maybe a few dates after that."

She folded her arms.

"It never went anywhere, but she, Michael, and I were so close we stuck together through today. It's been a while since we all got together."

"I see."

"*Stewardesses* helped keep the ties going."

Ashlyn nodded while she studied Jack's words and expression as he described his relationship with Sarah. She and Jack were still in the early phase of the relationship, and things were good... so far. She told herself, *Of course he's had other girlfriends. He isn't a monk, after all. It's fine.* But, the fact that Jack and Sarah were still in contact made her wonder a bit.

Jack cut another piece of trout. He paused for a moment. "More Broadway shows are coming to the Saenger soon. How about we get tickets?"

"Ooh yay! Anything catch your eye?"

"Not yet, but let's look and pick something."

"I'm just glad they finally reopened. Katrina was awhile back now, and it's too old and beautiful a theater venue to be just sitting there dormant."

"You're right. I know you're a nut for musical theater, so ladies choice."

Ashlyn smiled at Jack. She liked the spontaneous ideas he came up with for them. She reached for the wine bottle to pour another glass. She had finished her meal, and sat back in her chair while she eyed Jack warmly. Jack finished his food, and grabbed both their plates. He left them in the kitchen sink. Time enough for that later.

He refreshed his wine, and Ashlyn returned to the sofa. Jack turned her iPod on, and selected her romantic playlist. Soft music poured out of her iPod dock. Jack joined her back on the sofa.

Ashlyn said, "Make you a deal. We watch an episode of *Stewardesses* together if you watch a reality show with me."

Jack shifted a bit, "You're really pushing it now, huh?" He chuckled.

"It's fun! Okay, maybe they mix things around a bit. But it's interesting."

Jack smiled at her pleading her case.

"If you don't like it you don't have to watch again," Ashlyn laughed.

"Alright, same goes for you. Though you'll be hearing about it whenever you talk with Michael. He has the hots for one of the characters."

Ashlyn laughed. Jack set his glass down, caressing Ashlyn's face, saying, "Thanks for an amazing few months, baby. Looking forward to many more."

Ashlyn smiled and replied, "So am I, sweetheart."

He pulled her to him, kissing her as they laid back on the sofa, where the thoughts of Jack's ex girlfriend in Ashlyn's mind faded just a bit as they spent the night making love.

Chapter Six

Sarah was in the zone at Ales. She stood behind the bar, which boasted of seventy-five beers on tap, and almost as many available in bottles. Ales attracted a variety of people, from white-collar types on down to the guys who clocked out of Jiffy Lube, and grabbed a quick beer after work.

Sarah's jeans hugged her ample hips, and her tight Ales t-shirt was more than enough positive advertisement to the thirsty and willing males, and even the periodic females who lingered at the bar to get her attention. Her hair was cut short, and dyed a dark blue that bordered on purple. She got away with it at the bar, and the radio station tolerated it because she was a hard worker.

The main bar lined one wall, with the taps stretched out behind it like horses lined up for a race. Sarah and other regular bartenders knew where all the draft beers were by heart. She sometimes wondered if that was a good or bad thing.

Saturdays were one of their busiest nights. Sarah mostly worked weekends, so her weeknights were free for her boys. Thursdays were a compromise between her and the management, but they worked with her schedule, since she really ran a tight bar.

Of course, she also picked up a spare shift here and there during the week, or if she really needed the extra money.

As one bar patron got up and left, Sarah grabbed his empty glass, her tip, and wiped the area. Tips ranged from nothing to a few dollars. Beer was around $5 a glass and up, so the tips tended to be decent. Not always, of course.

She saw Michael as he came in the front door. Sarah met him with a hug, and he kissed her on the cheek.

"What's happening, girl?" he asked.

"The usual. Whatcha drinking tonight?"

"Sam Adams lager."

As Sarah fetched a glass, he glanced around. In addition to the long bar, Ales had tables and booths scattered about. Sarah put down Michael's beer, and he turned back toward the bar. "Jack should be on his way too," he told her.

"Oh good. So how about that *Stewardesses*?"

"Caught it online. Yeah... Good stuff."

"I know, right? Come on, heart attack mid flight?"

"Don't know what I'd do if that happened here, much less at 30,000 feet."

"And then making it out of Haiti in one piece with all the guys with guns shooting at them?"

"Thrill ride all the way. Been checking the Facebook group much?"

"When I can. Lots of Charlotte fans are on it."

"And this is surprising?" Michael took a sip of his beer. "So everything going alright?"

She rolled her eyes, and looked back at Michael. "Oh, the usual whirlwind. It ain't easy being me, ya know."

"Well, don't stop now."

"Somebody's got to do it, right?" She shuffled over to catch someone's refill at the far end of the bar. Michael returned to his beer.

A hand grabbed Michael's right shoulder. He heard Jack's voice say, "You got a lot of nerve coming here."

"Shut the hell up, Jack..." Michael turned, and both he and Jack smiled at one another. Michael asked, "So how goes it?"

"Not bad."

Michael looked over Jack's shoulder. "Ashlyn coming out?"

"Supposed to." Jack said, glancing around for her.

"Easy there, buddy."

"Yeah, definitely," Jack managed a smile, and glanced back to get Sarah's attention as she poured a few more beers for people.

Michael sipped his lager. "How's the online business hunt?"

"Trying that wholesale thing."

"Oh right, the sports website where you sell those jerseys and all?"

"Yep."

"And?"

"Ehh..."

"Sales?"

"Nope."

"Gotta be tough with people like Wal-Mart selling that crap for cheap."

Jack shrugged. "They say I need to promote it more. We'll see."

"Sounds right. I'm no guru, but look at Facebook and online in general. There's ass loads of website advertising all over the place."

Jack sat down on the barstool next to Michael.

"Yep. Gotta figure out my plan. I've been wasting a lot of money. Can't keep that up."

"Well, soon we'll be rolling in limo cash, so don't worry." Smiling, Michael took another sip of his beer.

"I'd settle for that." Jack nodded, smirking.

Michael raised his glass. "Working on it."

"Oh, on the limo business, got our insurance policy, but I need $600 from you for the premiums."

Michael nodded, "Um, okay. I'll let you know."

Sarah returned and said, "Hey, Jack. Your usual Fosters?"

Jack smiled at Sarah. "You read my mind."

She smirked. "You order so much as a Bass Ale, and I may drop dead."

"Ahh, guess you got me."

Sarah winked at Michael then spun toward the sea of taps. Jack grabbed Michael and asked, "Okay, what was that?"

"What was what?"

"The wink? Come on, man. We're best friends. Are you and Sarah...?"

Michael retorted with a frown, "We're just close, that's all. Kind of a brother-sister thing, you know."

"Yeaaah. I saw that look."

"So?"

"No brother checks his sister out like that."

"You're delusional. All this money talk is making you see things." Michael glanced away for a second. Jack doesn't even know about what happened. Can't tell him now... She'll hear it.

"Hey, man. You know I've been there."

"Yeah, yeah."

"She's hot. Wouldn't blame you."

"Nothing going on, okay?"

"Alright, alright. I just got a vibe on you two right then."

"A vibe? What the hell's that mean? There's no vibe—"

Sarah interrupted them, holding Jack's beer. "What about a vibe?"

As Jack opened his mouth to reply, Michael blurted out, "Oh, Jack was telling me about his favorite magazine. You know, Vibe?"

Sarah glanced at them a moment, replying, "Strange boys. Gotta switch out a keg, back in a few." She walked to the far end of the bar, through the door behind the beer tap lineup.

Jack shook his head at Michael. "Dude. Vibe magazine? That's the best you could think of?"

"As opposed to admitting I was checking her out?"

Jack slapped the bar. "So it IS true!"

"Let it go."

"You're a piece of work."

Michael sipped his beer. Jack asked, "How goes the apartment search?"

"Oh, I think my search is done."

"Yeah?"

"Got the B&G one."

"Thought you said it was occupado."

"Yeah, well it is. But let's just say Mr. Buddy likes the idea of more money. He's raised the rent, but with us splitting, it's more for him, but less than it was before for each person."

"Well damn, lucky bastards you are."

"The other tenant happens to be a relative of his. Sounds like he's doing the guy a favor. Divorce, down on his luck."

"Ahh. And you've only been a prized employee for how many years?"

"Guess they'd rather someone they already know, and it's not like they don't already know how much money I make."

"True that. Glad you got it all worked out."

"Least I can be out of your hair now."

Jack patted Michael's shoulder. "Love ya bro, but soon you'll put a crimp on my love life."

"Don't throw it in my face, okay? Is she coming or not?"

Jack arched an eyebrow at Michael's word choice. Michael shook his head, trying to hide a grin. "All right, all right!"

Laughing, Jack said, "She's supposed to call me any time now."

Sarah came back with Jack's beer. Michael raised his empty glass. "Who do I have to kill to get a beer around here?"

She snatched the glass from Michael's hand. "I will beat your ass in front of all the women here."

Michael and Jack responded with yelps and shouts of excitement. Michael gestured toward Sarah, and announced to the others at the bar, "There she is, ladies and gentlemen, my friend, Sarah. Pours a mean beer, and puts you in your place without breaking a sweat." Michael bowed in mock adulation as Jack and a few others nearby laughed and applauded.

"Sit down, smart-ass. Here's your beer. So, have I missed anything on the *Stewardesses* Facebook page?"

Jack replied, "Looks like they're pulling the plug soon."

"Oh no! Just like that? Why don't they give it time?"

"Dunno. I'd think the internet buzz would mean something to them." Michael said.

Sarah asked, "Can anything be done?"

"There's several 'Save *Stewardesses*' web sites cropping up now. I'm taking a look at them." Michael replied.

Jack said, "Big shame if it's canceled."

Sarah asked, "What about the shows left to air? Any tidbits

about that?"

"Just the usual chatter," Michael replied. "Theories about Monique and Tim getting together. Monique might start searching for her long lost brother. We'll see what happens."

Sarah collected empty glasses from the bar as she listened. "I guess Monique is going to be the number one focus now. The romance is fine, but I want more action like the Haiti episode."

"Hear hear," Michael chimed in. "If I wanted drama, I'd watch daytime talk shows."

Jack's mobile phone rang. Seeing Ashlyn's name, he smiled, and went outside. "Hey, babe, I'm at Ales with Jack and Sarah. Coming by?"

"Be there in about ten minutes."

"Okay, see you then!"

Jack put his phone away, and returned to the bar. "Alright, she's on her way."

"Great!" Michael said.

Sarah said, "So did she get into *Stewardesses*?"

"No, she likes reality shows." Jack shrugged.

Wincing, Michael leaned in toward Jack, "Reality shows? Like the one about people getting voted off an island?"

"More like the Annoying Desperate Psychotic Housewives," Jack answered.

Michael cringed. He didn't care for so-called "reality television," but Ashlyn was cool enough.

Feeling a burn in his stomach from hunger, Michael ordered some chili cheese fries. He glanced down at his beer glass, thinking. *Eating bar food. Okay, that tastes good. I mean, it's Ales food after all.* But here he was, alone. With his friends, yes. And he'd been here probably thousands of nights already, in pretty much this exact spot. And what would there be ahead for him? The limo business, if it took off. But what if it didn't? Was this his future: himself at 50 or older, a man who checked out college girls who were young enough to be his daughters? He wondered what he could add to his life to make it feel less mundane.

Whatever it is better happen soon, Michael thought. *Can't live the rest of my life like this, waiting for things to change on their own. I need some kind of cause to work for, a direction to go in, a career maybe. And I don't think it will come from one of dad's ideas either. Dad never seemed all that happy, either.* Michael considered the people who worked on the crews for producing TV shows, and what it would take to be one of them. That seemed like a decent way to spend time. Certainly better than the cash register bit.

Michael looked back up at Jack. "I just want to feel like I'm heading somewhere, you know?"

"You eat all those chili fries, and you'll be heading... to the can." Jack laughed.

Michael rolled his eyes at Jack, and Jack quickly added, "Hey dude, buck up. I'm gonna keep looking at News On Wheels ads, they're bound to get a car we like."

"Sure, why not?"

Jack nodded. "Did you set up a Facebook page for the limos, get the high school dance kids?"

"Yeah. Oh and I have a lead already. Niece of Ms. Rose, needs a ride for her and another couple Saturday, October 13th."

"Sweet! So a little over two weeks to get us a car. Totally doable." Jack smiled, and leaned in to add, "Look, maybe you can get a better job for now, too. Ya know, til we get the limos going good?"

"Got something in mind?"

"Quicksolve is always looking for people."

"No degree, remember?"

"Doesn't matter, you have some college."

"Doing tech support? Hmm, I dunno."

"Just think about it."

Michael took a swallow of beer as Sarah returned. "So Sarah, how's the rough and tumble world of radio?"

"Oh, it's a wonderland," Sarah retorted. "I have the most understanding boss, and, in fact, I'm due for a promotion to management any day now. Seriously," she added, dropping the sarcasm, "Peter gives me hell, but that's nothing new."

"Like what?"

"Just, getting time to deal with the boys' immunization records was a small miracle. And, oh yeah, the boys are still getting into their own trouble."

43

"What now?"

"Sneaking into the girls bathroom. Really? Is this what they learned from their father? Oh wait, he wasn't around. So where the hell did they get this?" She shook her head.

Michael and Jack looked at each other. "Damn, that's rough."

"Mmmhmm," She replied, playing with a stack of coasters. "So those radio bastards better make good with the concert tickets."

"Still pining for Dave Grohl, are we?"

She batted her eyes. "What do you think?"

Someone signaled for Sarah a few feet down the bar. As she side skipped over to them, Michael turned back to Jack and said softly, "See? I can't be with Sarah. I'm not a rock star."

Jack smiled, and clinked his glass against Michael's. Suddenly they heard Sarah deadpan, "Holy shit." They saw Sarah with her mouth agape, eyes fixed on the entrance to Ales. They turned to see a girl with long blonde hair that cascaded about her shoulders. Her skin tight jeans looked like she was sewn into them. Her shirt showed a little of her midriff and the hint of a tattoo.

"There she is," Jack said, as he welcomed her with a hug and kiss.

"Forgot how she likes to dress for a night out," Michael whispered to Sarah.

Sarah held her gaze, but nodded to Michael. "I'd hit that."

Jack brought Ashlyn over. "Remember these guys?"

"Of course, how are you?"

Michael reached out to hug her. "Eh, can't complain."

Ashlyn smiled at Michael. "Heard you've gotten into that *Stewardesses* show."

Michael eyed Jack. "Did you now?"

Jack shrugged. Michael continued, "Yeah, a bit. Among other things."

"Caught a few minutes of it last week," she looked at Jack with a smile.

Jack replied, "Glad we could do this again. Been awhile since we'd been here, right babe?"

Ashlyn slid onto a bar chair. "Yeah, for sure. We've been staying more uptown for the nightlife." She scanned the bar area.

Michael studied the couple for a moment. He turned to Ashlyn and asked, "Care for a drink?"

Ashlyn glanced at Jack, who said, "Yeah, damn, um... Ashlyn needs a..."

"Merlot," whispered Ashlyn.

"Merlot, Sarah!"

Sarah took another moment to stare, then grabbed a wine bottle. When she brought Ashlyn her wine, she said, "Lemme know if ya need help with these fools."

"Sure," Ashlyn smiled at the offer. Sarah's look was a far cry from the business types and sorority sisters Ashlyn was used to. Still, she had managed to get used to Sarah a little. Enough that she handled being around her now and then, anyway. Now she figured, if Jack saw enough in Sarah to date her, she should at least try to be polite.

Sarah left them to handle another order. Jack handed Ashlyn her merlot. She took a sip and asked, "So what have I missed?"

Jack replied, "Usual chitchat. The latest on *Stewardesses*, of course."

Michael added, "Evaluating where we are, career-wise and personally. Next up, that curing cancer thing."

Smirking and nodding, she replied, "I see." "Still at the grocery store?"

Michael's shoulders slumped a bit. "Yeah."

"How's that going?"

"It's all right, I guess. Steady work until I find something better, or the limos take off."

"Oh right."

"Need a ride in style?"

Ashlyn chuckled, "Um no, but thanks."

"Worth a shot," Michael shrugged.

"Good luck with that. And hey, I worked a lot of part-time jobs before I landed my accounting gig."

"Pays a lot?"

She nodded. "Decent money."

"Nights and weekends off?"

"Yep, except for the occasional business function. Gives me more time to spend with this guy," Ashlyn said as she playfully ran her hand through Jack's hair.

45

Jack glanced at her affectionately. "That's the true challenge."

Michael chimed in, "I don't need to worry about becoming wealthy, not when my good friend Jack here is hell-bent on creating his own business, solving the world's problems and becoming filthy rich. Right, buddy?" He patted Jack on the back.

Taking a sip of his beer, Jack replied, "For now, I'm just trying to make back the money I've lost."

At that moment, Sarah walked over to the group with Michael's chili cheese fries. "Okay guys, dig in!" She set the plate on the bar between Michael and Jack, then motioned to Ashlyn to help herself. "Don't let these vultures have all the fun," she quipped.

Michael grabbed a fry, pulling it from the pile. Cheese stretched in several strands, and chili slowly slid down, some of it splashing onto the plate. He immediately popped the fry into his mouth. The heat of the cheese and fries were a bit too much, so he grabbed his beer, and took a large gulp to wash the fry down.

Jack looked at him with a mix of amusement and mild disgust. Ashlyn asked, "You alright?"

Once he had swallowed the beer, Michael replied, "I'm fine. I just love the chili cheese fries here. You guys want some?"

Jack responded, "Yeah. Babe?" He turned to Ashlyn.

"No thanks," Ashlyn replied with a hint of disgust. She sipped her wine and tried to keep her eyes averted from the rabid feast before her.

After he gave the fries a little longer to cool, Michael dug back in, and savored the salty meatiness of the chili with the cheese and fries.

As Sarah brought the next round of drinks, she asked, "How's the Help Desk, Jack?"

"Not bad. I like the solving computer problems part, you know?"

"But don't some people get bitchy?"

"Well yeah."

"I don't know how you put up with all that. I've heard those tech support nightmare calls on YouTube."

"I deal with techno-phobic people, that's for sure."

"I prefer my customers more or less drunk," Sarah smiled, gesturing to them.

Jack shrugged, "Once had a guy swear his wireless mouse was broken. Turned out to be a dead battery."

"I would have had to get his address and go smack him."

"Long weekends and overtime shifts suck. But could be worse -- I could be doing telemarketing or something."

Sarah nodded, "Sure beats the hell out of some people I deal with." She lowered her voice to add, "I bust my ass here Fridays and Saturdays, and some of these losers don't tip at all or--worse-- leave me pennies."

As he listened to Sarah and Jack complain, Michael wondered out loud, "If you guys aren't happy with your jobs, why aren't you looking for new ones?"

Almost as one, they turned to face him. Sarah crossed her arms and said, "Well that's something, coming from the guy who's still making minimum wage at the grocery store."

"I'm just saying if you're unhappy, there's other jobs."

Sarah said, "Yeah, I know that. I just get tired of people telling me what I should be doing. Especially if they aren't exactly setting the world on fire, either."

"Calm down. Hey, I'm getting things going."

"Oh, the limo service?"

Michael squared up a bit. "Yeah, Jack and I. And if not that, something else will happen."

"Something else, like dropping out of college?"

"I'm having a hard time settling on something."

"Settling on something, my ass. You lived the life on your mom and dad's nickel, for how long was it?"

Michael's chest tightened. "Well you settled for a great guy. Real father figure. Tell me again, where is he now?"

Sarah's eyes began to well up as she glared at Michael. Her face reddened. "Don't you... have to be... getting up for work tomorrow?" She huffed.

Ashlyn lowered her glass, glancing at Jack.

Jack jumped in, "It's getting late. How about we do this again soon?" He looked at Ashlyn, who nodded.

Michael replied, "Okay fine. Sarah, I'm sorry."

Sarah held her scowl, pretended to hear someone calling from the far side of the bar, and stalked away, but not before she shot back a glare in Michael's direction.

"You always had a way with the ladies," Jack patted Michael on his shoulder.

Sarah closed out Jack and Michael's tabs. After they paid, Jack said goodnight, and headed out the door with his arm around Ashlyn. Michael lingered as Sarah wiped up at the far end of the bar.

"Hey, Sarah?" he called out.

No acknowledgment.

He tried again, "Didn't mean to-"

She just pointed to the door. He shuffled out of the bar.

He tried calling her, back at Jack's apartment, but it just went to voicemail. *Great. I've gotta watch that, he thought. Too easy to rile me up, and that wasn't anything she deserved.*

Chapter Seven

As far as apartments went, the one behind B&G was more cramped than anything Michael could imagine. He'd caught glimpses of the old building over the months he'd worked at the grocery, but he'd never seen the inside until moving in.

Michael peered at his laptop while he sat at the kitchen table. He posted to the JM Limos Facebook page, and checked what was going on with the *Stewardesses* group.

"Damn, you looking at that thing again? You got a porn fix or something?"

Brad, his new roommate, was a little more than he'd bargained for.

"Whadya want?" Michael asked.

"Hey you wanna waste time online, go ahead."

"Mmhmm."

"Don't forget taking that shit out to the trash."

Michael squinted. "What're you talking about?"

"You know, the garbage that's been there for a few days under the sink? I'm not your goddamn maid."

"What about you?"

"Yeah, well I've been working late a lot, and handling this place just fine before you moved here."

Refocused on his laptop, Michael sighed, "Okay, I'll take care of it today."

"Alright. Oh yeah, rent's due next week. Gonna need your half by Friday."

His eyes still on the screen, Michael murmured, "Got it."

Brad slammed the door, headed off to his job, whatever it was. Being an asshole to people, Michael mused. Brad was wrong about the garbage, Michael remained behind taking plenty of trash out right after he'd moved in. He'd only been there two weeks, and he'd even cooked a few times already. He figured Brad was just pissed about whatever his ex or life in general had done to him.

Whatever the case, it wasn't his big concern today. He and Jack were going to check out and maybe buy a car to get their limo service off and running. He felt like a kid about to open his presents on Christmas morning. Jack was supposed to head over on his lunch hour, and Michael was just waiting for the word to meet him.

Michael's phone vibrated on the table.

"JM Limos, where you roll like a star."

"Clever, Michael. That's our slogan?"

"Maybe."

"Keep trying."

"So you ready to do this?"

Michael picked up one of the full trash bags. "Few more minutes and I can leave."

"Alright, meet you there!"

***

Michael and Jack examined the long, black Town Car. The salesman had wandered off to strike up a conversation with some other Tuesday shoppers while they mulled their purchase over like the US Federal Budget.

"Well, what do you think?" Michael asked.

Jack shrugged, "Alright to me. Whatcha think?"

Michael walked around the car. Out of the corner of his eye, he caught the salesman who had spoken with them. They watched him as he gesticulated rather furiously at a customer. "What do ya make of him?"

"Just a used car salesman."

"I didn't wear ties that bad when it was Halloween."

"If he'd just shut up more." Jack chuckled.

"Yeah, those sales guys give me the creeps."

Jack nodded, and eyed the car again. "It's their way."

"And my dad wanted me to do sales." Michael scoffed. "Let's see about a test drive, so we don't spend twelve grand on a car that burns oil tomorrow or something."

Michael climbed into the back seat. "So Sarah sent me an email."

"Yeah?"

"First time since that night."

"Still pissed?"

"Oh yeah, for sure. I screwed up."

"Yep."

"I got flustered, man. Besides, I can't figure out her and Jimmy. He's used and abused her, but she just won't shut him out completely."

"Never that simple when there's kids."

"Yeah, guess not. They just... need something better."

"Least you're talking again."

They waved the salesman Todd over. He approached them, grinning a little too much. "So, we ready to pull the trigger on this one?"

"Almost. We'd like a test drive first."

"Hmm, we can do that. Wasn't sure at first if you wanted to buy it or sleep with it the way you were fawning," he tapped Michael on the shoulder. "I'm only kidding. Lemme get the keys from the shop, and I'll be right back."

Michael glanced at Jack. "If it weren't for this car I'd have punched him by now."

Jack laughed. "And that's why I'm handling the money."

"Well fine. This is gonna be good, man. I feel it."

"If we get this going right, we could get a crew working for us. More cars too."

"I've been getting some feedback on Facebook about the dances for the fall, so I think we can get a few weekends booked."

Jack nodded. "We could get some airport jobs too. Maybe."

"Oh yeah?" Michael leaned back on the car.

"I have an uncle who works at Armstrong International."

"Celebs?"

"You're not gonna be driving Brad Pitt around, but maybe an exec or two."

"Runs from airport to hotels?"

"Pretty much."

"I could probably fit that in with my B&G schedule."

"Exec jobs are choice. High school dances are nice, but more competition."

"At least we have the one tonight all set, if we can close this deal."

Jack patted Michael's back. "See? It's happening."

Michael shrugged. "Sooner I can get something going, quit B&G, and move away from Mr. Dickhead, the better."

"How's that going so far?"

Michael laughed. "I'm beginning to see why the guy is divorced. Dude lives like a slob. And damn, I don't expect you to be all cheery, but don't chew my head off for nothing. At least he works long hours and nights several times a week."

"Hey, it's a place to stay. Maybe a little motivation to get JM Limos rocking too?"

"Sure thing."

***

Michael eased the Town Car onto Clearview Parkway early Saturday evening, headed toward I-10. He glanced in the rear-view at his four passengers, who chatted with each other.

"Everybody comfy?" Michael asked.

"Doing fine," answered the girl in the red dress. That was Ms. Rose's niece, Chloe.

Michael nodded. "Well good. So how y'all know each other?"

Chloe replied, "Well, Jamie and I were in Girl Scouts together."

"Ahh I see. Well y'all look nice. Sure you'll have a great

52

time."

One of the guys piped in, "Hey can we stop off on the way back at a convenience store or something?"

"What for?" Michael asked.

"Oh, just something," he replied, a slight smile on his lips.

Michael eyed him in the mirror. "We'll see."

He pulled the car up to the Pontchartrain Hotel on St. Charles Avenue. Jumping out, he opened the door to let the girls and their dates out. "All right, you guys. Have a good time, I'll be back around 10."

Chloe said, "Thanks, Michael," and they turned to enter the hotel.

Michael checked the dashboard clock. It was 8:15pm. He had a little time to kill, but not enough for a stroll around the French Quarter. He figured on a Barq's Root Beer at Camellia Grill as a better option.

The car's radiator had other plans.

He didn't notice the dashboard indicator at first. He'd driven a few minutes, and then he caught it at a red light.

"Shit."

He turned the car off and on again, no change. Michael always made sure the needle got to the "E" in any car he drove, but beyond gasoline he was a loss on how this kind of issue was handled. He checked his phone, and headed to the nearest Pep Boys, on S. Carrollton. So much for a cold one. He pulled into Pep Boys lot, and smiled a bit as he noticed the Mandarin House restaurant next door, a favorite of his parents when he was growing up.

After a few minutes inside Pep Boys, Michael ended up with a few bottles of antifreeze and some Radiator Stop Leak. He asked the manager for a little help with the radiator repairs, and the manager said it would just be a minute.

Back outside, Michael popped the hood, and then heard a very familiar voice call his name.

He turned quickly. "Hey dad."

John approached cautiously. "Hey, son. Um, how are you?"

He studied his dad for a moment.

"I'm fine. How're you?"

"Good, Mom and I are eating next door. I came out to grab a

smoke and saw - did you buy a Lincoln Town Car?"

"Yeah, I did. Me and Jack. Limo business, remember?"

A smile crept onto John's face. "You did it."

"Well so far just part time."

"I'm really glad to hear that. You have time to step in next door? Your mom would love to see you."

"Maybe a few minutes. But I need to take care of this radiator. I have a customer to pick up in about an hour."

"Well let me give you a hand," John said, slipping his cigarette back in the pack.

After they fixed up the car, he followed his dad into the restaurant. As they walked up behind Barbara, John quipped, "Ya never know who'll end up in this place."

Barbara turned her head, slight surprise on her face. "Well, well. Good to see you. What brings you here?"

"Well, dad," Michael replied. "Car trouble."

"What happened?"

"Radiator problems."

"Aww well maybe your dad can help."

"He did."

John nodded, smiling.

Barbara continued, "You doing okay otherwise?"

"I'm fine, I guess."

"Please sit, you want to get something? We just ordered a few minutes ago."

"No, no, I can't stay too long. I'm um-"

"-He's on the clock," John said. "Working for himself."

"Is that so?" Barbara replied. "Your limo company? What was it called again?"

"JM Limos. Yeah. Still at the grocery too. But we're getting some response now. I even have a few leads on picking people up at the airport. Jack and I are working at it."

"Well that's great," Barbara smiled.

"What about that car?" John asked. "Looks good on the outside, but you'd better get that radiator looked at. Filling a leaky one just prolongs the problem."

"I know, all right. We're just trying to do all this without breaking the bank." Michael replied.

"Well don't break your car either," John said.

Michael nodded. A waiter joined them at the table. "Will there be three now?"

"No, I just stopped by for a moment," Michael said, standing up. The waiter nodded and left.

"It really is good to see you both," Michael said. "I'm sorry for how things went the night I left home. I was wrong, you were right. I broke the deal we had, and you were keeping me honest."

John and Barbara glanced at each other. "We love you, Michael, just keep pushing forward. Okay? Come and see us sometime."

Michael smiled. "I will. Love you both too." And he took off back to the Pontchartrain.

***

Laughter and chatter emanated from the back seat as Michael drove his happy dance attendees home. He wondered if he and Jack had sounded like that back in the day when they hit up the dance scene back then.

"Can you believe Tina?" Jamie said.

Chloe replied, "She just won't quit."

"She needs to get another guy, and stay away from mine."

"It's drama," Chloe replied. "It's no fun for her unless she has an audience. Think she would've pulled that shit if we weren't all at a public dance?"

"Um, yeah."

"Maybe. I think she wanted to make you squirm in public."

"Fail."

Michael asked, "So I'm just dropping you all back at your house, Chloe, or what?"

The inquisitive kid leaned up, his hand on Jack's seat. "How about the convenience store first?"

Michael paused a moment, then replied, "Yeah, sure. Can't wait until tomorrow?"

"Naah, just a little something I - uh we needed to get."

Michael heard Chloe speak to the boy, saying, "Kyle, what's so important about stopping off, exactly?"

55

"It's a surprise," Kyle remarked.

Chloe scoffed, but quickly switched gears and asked Jamie, "Did you see the latest episode?"

"Yes!" Jamie gasped. "I can't believe Monique and the pilot finally got together!"

"Oh what? Like they weren't gonna from the start."

Michael beamed at the name recognition. "Hey, y'all watch *Stewardesses* too?"

Jamie replied, "Um yes. You know it?"

"You could say that. I'm a fan."

"No kidding."

"Been following it on TV and Facebook."

A pause from the back. Chloe said, "Really, didn't think guys watched that show."

"Just 'cause they aren't in bikinis doesn't mean they aren't good to look at." Michael chuckled. "They have good plots too. Hope they keep the show going."

"That's a chick show," the other boy in the back remarked.

"Shush, Justin." Jamie said. "It's a good show, and anyone can watch it if they want."

"Y'all should check out the Facebook group for the show. They have petitions for trying to save it and all." Michael said. "Looks like the network might cancel it."

"Huh. Well that'd be a shame. I'll check that out," Chloe replied.

***

Michael pulled into the Exxon at the corner of Clearview and Veterans. There were few cars at the pumps, and a couple of late night patrons wandered the aisles of food and beer inside.

"Can we talk to you a minute?" Kyle asked Michael, as he opened the door.

Michael glanced at Chloe, she shrugged. "Alright." He exited the car to see Kyle and Justin. They motioned away from the car, and he walked over to stand by the side of the store with them.

"What?" Michael asked.

Kyle and Justin looked at each other a moment, both of them

mouthed some words Michael couldn't make out, and gestured toward him until finally Kyle spoke. "Hey, we were just wondering if you'd buy us a bottle of something in there."

"Alcohol." Michael replied.

"Yeah. I have the money, just... well it'd be really cool and all."

Michael's mind skipped back again to high school, him and Jack's dalliances with underage drinking. Yeah, it was fun at the time. But getting caught wasn't.

He glanced at the car. The girls watched them. *Even if Chloe wasn't related to my boss, this just doesn't seem like a good idea.*

Michael turned to Justin and Kyle. Kyle held a wad of crumpled bills out, a hopeful smile on his face.

"Guys, I'm not doing this. If this is all we came here for, it's not gonna happen."

"Aww come on dude," Justin said. "Help us out."

"No, not me. Sorry," Michael shook his head, nodding back to the car.

He started to walk when Kyle grabbed his shoulder. "You said you'd help us out, man. This isn't cool."

"Cool?" Michael retorted, swiveling his shoulder away from him. "I'm doing y'all a favor. Okay? From me. Might seem shitty now. But trust me, you aren't gonna like what happens. You might for awhile, sure."

Kyle and Justin looked at each other, turning their annoyed gaze back at Michael.

Michael continued, "What do y'all plan on doing back at the house? Think you might even get a little something off one of these girls? Just don't. Not like this. Trust me. Not the right way." He turned again to walk back to the car.

"This is bullshit," Justin said, walking up behind Michael. Who the hell you think you are?"

Michael lunged back at Justin, getting in his face. "Someone with an alcoholic in his family, okay? Someone who got into trouble for underage drinking in high school. I dropped out of college because I couldn't keep it together to think, much less study and pass tests. I used to be you, asshole. And now I'm trying to catch up everything I've been missing because I was too hammered

57

to think straight. Trying to help you out here, alright?"

Kyle stepped between them. "Okay, okay, it's cool. Let's just get back home. It's fine." He pocketed the wad of bills.

Justin glared at Michael, and then glanced at Kyle. "Whatever."

They got back in the car, and left the convenience store parking lot in silence.

"What was all that about?" Jamie asked.

"Some man talk," Michael commented.

Chapter Eight

"The radiator's bad?"

"Yeah, the light came on Saturday night during that dance job."

Jack leaned back in his cubicle with his eyes closed. He tried thoughts of something serene, anything... Ashlyn and him in bed, an overseas flight with foot rubs by the *Stewardesses*, anything.

After a few moments, he sat up again. "Okay. We get it fixed."

"Pep Boys said it would probably be around $500."

"There goes our first profits." Jack sighed.

"It's gonna be fine. Look, we have those airport runs we can do, right?"

"Maybe, if my uncle calls me back."

"I can call too. During the day and all."

"We'll see," Jack said as he scratched his temples. "He's touchy about people harassing him."

"I'll be gentle," Michael chuckled. "Why not? We're a team, right? JM baby!"

"Okay. Hey, til we get JM baby doing more, how about the other job?"

"Working with your tech support deal?"

"Yeah, I'll get you an interview. Pays more than whatcha got now."

"You think I could do that work?"

"Much as you do on Facebook, absolutely."

"Alright, I'm convinced. What do I do?"

"Send your resume. I'll get you a link."

"Yeah, on that resume thing. Can you help me out?"

Jack sighed. "Uh I guess?"

"How 'bout tomorrow?"

"Mmmm, that should be okay."

"Alright. I'll get dinner. Thanks a bunch!"

"No good deed..." Jack muttered as he turned back to his support tickets.

***

Michael and Jack sat on Jack's couch, Michael's laptop on the coffee table in front of them. They stared at it like painters with a blank canvas.

"Key to tell them what you can do without saying too much," Jack explained.

"How long did yours take to do?" Michael asked.

Scratching his head, Jack thought a moment. "Had mine since college and just kinda tweaked since, so... few hours maybe?"

"Can't imagine mine's gonna take that long," Michael sighed.

"Still gotta figure out how we make your 'experience' sound good."

"You mean 'bullshit'?"

Jack chuckled. "I guess. Any way, you need this to get the job. It's kinda a sales pitch."

"Oh, sales, now ya tell me. My dad would be all about this."

"Right?"

Michael smiled at Jack. "One day we won't need to worry about sending resumes, huh?"

"Maybe. I'm better at losing money these days."

Michael sat up. "What happened with your website? Get your money back?"

"We'll see. Even canceling the account is a bitch."

"Damn. See, hearing that makes me not want to even try."

Jack grabbed his arm. "Except for the limos."

"Yeah, of course."

"And come on, gotta put yourself out there now and then."

Jack grabbed a notepad and paper. He set them down beside the laptop. "It's bad, but I've done bad deals before. Just gotta keep trying. So, on to that resume."

Michael leaned back on the sofa and sighed. "I dunno, man."

"What's wrong?"

"You really think this is right for me? I mean, I can operate a computer, but I don't know if I'm cut out for tech support."

Jack sat down on the sofa next to Michael. "You kidding? All the times you logged on to Facebook to drool electronically over Charlotte Ducrest? And that Twitter role playing thing?"

Michael scratched his head. "Yeah, well, I'm the king of wasting time."

"You also helped people on Facebook with uploading files or online polls on the *Stewardesses* Facebook page."

"That's true."

"What makes you think what I do in tech support is so much different than that?"

Michael nodded. "Guess I hadn't thought about it like that. But what am I supposed to put down on this resume, 'Helps people worship TV actresses better online? Role plays on Twitter like few can?'"

Jack sighed. "Gotta take a chance, to see if it's right. You might get this job... more money, more options."

Michael absorbed the idea. "Okay, fine, what first?"

"We order food, and hammer out this baby."

"Alright. Lead the way, Jack. I'm in your hands."

As Michael picked up the phone to call Papa John's, Jack grabbed his flash drive. Michael plopped back down on the sofa with two bottles of root beer. Handing one to Jack, he said, "Here... brain food."

Jack connected his flash drive to the laptop, and opened his own resume file. "See, HR looks at resumes all damn day. We have to get their attention."

Michael nodded. Jack continued. "We'll need to get a little creative on yours..."

"So we're back to bullshit?"

Jack was incredulous. "Stop saying that. We'll put down jobs you worked. We need as many as you remember."

"So B&G Grocery?"

"It's a job, they hired you, you worked there. Gotta start with something."

"Alright."

"Then we show your computer skills. All what you did with Facebook, even Twitter."

"Okay."

"We're using all that. It isn't lying if you've done it."

Michael nodded. "All right, let's see what I can remember about my work history."

Michael recounted all the jobs he'd worked, as Jack typed away. Turns out there had been several more before B&G Grocery.

Michael was surprised when he glanced over his entire known work history, laid out in front of him for the first time on one screen. He had more jobs than he'd thought, though not one of them led to the next. College friends of his had progressed further though, and many of them were well into their careers. *At least I've been working on a steady basis*, he thought to himself.

Michael glanced at Jack and said, "Okay, that's all of them. Now what?"

Jack replied, "Now we figure out how to say you're the guy for helping people on computers."

A knock on the door. Jack said, "But first, there's the important matter of pizza!"

Michael grabbed his wallet, and headed for the door. "Payment for services rendered."

They ate pizza, and drank beer at the kitchen table. Michael tried to lighten the mood a bit. "Heard from Sarah?"

"Not since we had drinks at Ales."

Michael said, "We should hang out there more often."

Jack replied, "Yeah, I think Ashlyn would be up for that."

"How are y'all doing?"

"We're alright--mostly. She's been pushing for more time together. She's feeling neglected."

"Uh oh, gotta watch that, man. How long have you been together now?"

Jack paused a moment. "Little over six months."

"Don't want her bored and looking elsewhere!" Michael teased.

Jack laughed, "I'll have more free time on my hands now without that website."

"At least you tried."

Jack nodded. "Yep. And I will again."

"I need to do more."

"Just keep regrouping and pushing ahead."

"Hey, at least you're trying, Jack. That's more than people like me can say."

"Enough of this pity party. You're taking positive steps." Jack tapped the laptop screen and the beginning of Michael's resume.

They went back to work. Jack added several items under work experience, how Michael was good at helping friends with problems on Facebook and other websites. Before long, the resume was finished. Jack displayed it on the screen, and slid the laptop over to Michael, saying, "Have a look at it; it's your baby."

Michael glanced at the resume. His resume. He felt... oddly different. In the short time they had worked on this, nothing had changed. But, the finished document gave him a sense of accomplishment. Now he had a chance at better jobs making more money. Maybe this was the push he needed. Maybe this would get him on the right track.

Michael looked at Jack and said, "It's great, man! Thank you so much." He placed a hand on Jack's shoulder.

Jack patted Michael's extended arm. "This is just Part One. I'll email it to you with a link. Send it in and, with a little luck, they'll contact you for an interview."

Michael clasped his hands. "Okay, sure thing."

"You have dress clothes?"

Michael shifted, and groaned a bit. "I have a blazer and slacks."

"There's hope for you yet. Tie?"

Michael stared.

Jack shook his head. "Okay, for the interview you can borrow one."

Michael looked again at his resume. He tried not to dwell on the rift between him and his parents. It bothered him still, but he was glad he made this move for a career.

Michael asked Jack, "So what do you think my chances are?"

Jack replied, "Well, they're willing to train, and give people a shot if they feel they're right for the job."

"And how would I fit?"

Jack leaned back for a moment. "I think you've got a fair chance; just get this in soon."

They shut down the laptop, and sat back on the sofa to watch TV. Michael asked Jack, "Any words of advice, for getting an interview?"

Jack kept his eyes on the TV, but smiled and pondered the question before he said, "Don't be a smart-ass, but be persistent and not annoying."

Michael looked at Jack, and held out his beer to toast him. "Here's to you, Jack. For helping me get onto that corporate ladder."

Jack smiled, and brought his bottle to clink Michael's. He replied, "Let's hold off on the thank-you's until you actually get it. Glad I could help so far."

***

Michael hung around another half hour before taking off. Jack felt good that he helped his friend get another step further along, maybe to an actual career. He laughed to himself as he sat on his couch, and swirled his bottle around.

Whenever the subject of careers came up, he often thought about his dad, and all he went through and faced. Jack grabbed the phone.

"Dad?" Jack asked.

"Hey son," the voice sounded tired, as usual.

"How was work?"

"Ah, had another delivery come through today. Canned goods this time."

Jack winced. "You didn't lift those heavy boxes, did you?"

"No, no, I'm fine. They know my limits, and they chip in."

"You sure?"

Jack's dad laughed. "Yeah, son. But ya know I'm not a feeble old man yet."

"You're almost 70. Just don't want you in the hospital."

"It's alright. I know, son. I appreciate the concern. So, enough about me. How're you doing?"

"Not bad. Me and Michael got our first client for that limo service."

"Hey, sounds great!" His next words broke off into coughing. "You should come and pick me up sometime, I could use a ride like that."

Jack laughed. "Sure dad. Gonna try and get some airport business through Uncle Chuck soon."

"Oh good. Well keep it up, son. Proud of what you're doing there."

Jack's beaming feeling was tempered by worry. It wasn't like his dad wanted a job at Wal-Mart at his age, of course. Jack hoped his dad could've quit at 68, but it just wasn't meant to be. Between social security and Jack's mom's death, there wasn't much of a choice.

"Dad, I'm gonna get you set up, somehow. Gonna work on getting you free of that job."

"Aww son. Take care of yourself first, alright? I'd rather know you're going to be alright before me."

"Working at it."

"How's Ashlyn?"

"She's great, how about we take you out for lunch this weekend?"

"That sounds good. Maybe out in West End somewhere?"

Jack found it harder to choke back the emotion the longer the conversation went. Just thoughts of his dad, a worker past retirement age at one of the few jobs he qualified for, a grocery stocker, was tough on him. His dad was always the one in charge, the man with a plan. Jack hated how things turned for his dad. Whenever he hesitated or doubted his own business efforts, his father's example just screamed out to him why he couldn't quit.

There was no way he'd let that be what happened to him.

Jack bit his lip and said, "You got it, dad. Anywhere you want to go."

Chapter Nine

Sarah sat in her cubicle at WZEB-FM. So far, it was a typical
Monday. Sarah's salary wasn't great, but the perks and little extras
made it worth hanging around.

Peter was not a "perk." Of course, he had his moments of
generosity, however few and far apart they might be. Whether
people admired, tolerated, or loathed Peter, no one could deny he
had a way with words. He just somehow made people forget they
dealt with someone who sold to them. He was also quite the life of
the party. At station Holiday celebrations and even some live
broadcasts, Peter was the guy surrounded by people as he told
jokes, fishing stories or something similar.

His charm never worked on Sarah, but he liked her anyway.
Whenever forced to give a reason, he said he admired her
tenacity... then added a crude comment about her appearance.

It was mid morning, and the sales people had left to make their
daily calls. Sarah called the automated number for her credit card
balance. She wanted that productive feeling she did something
about the bill, even if it was just the knowledge of how much she
owed.

While she was on the phone, Peter called out, "Hey Sarah, need you to come here quick." Sighing, Sarah hung up, grabbed a notepad and pen, and walked slowly into Peter's office. She never knew what to expect when he called her in. Sometimes he handed her a rough copy of a new sales piece. Other times, he wanted to tell her about some hunting trip he'd been on or some crazy night out with his buddies. Then there were times he asked if a particular salesperson slacked off.

As she entered Peter's office, Sarah saw he was glancing at the day's newspaper. "Morning," she said.

After a few more seconds, Peter looked up. "Hey! Good morning, Sarah. Listen, I've created a new sales package for this coming week. It's a little lengthy, so I need you to start on it right away."

Sarah nodded. "What's this one about?"

Peter replied, "You'll see. We're doing a comparison of radio, television, and newspaper advertising. We're trying to entice businesses to switch their advertising over to us. Way I see it, we aren't going after all the business we can, and this should change that."

Sarah nodded, and wrote a few notes on her pad. These proposals were something she enjoyed, for the most part, though the back-and-forth over word choice--Peter as he always changed his mind about phrasing--drove her nuts. However, she took a lot of pride in that she was the one who laid out the proposal, and made it look nice. It was the best part of this job, like joking and flirting with Ales patrons was her favorite part of that job.

Sarah glanced down at her notes, then back at Peter. "Is that it?"

Peter replied, "For now. Oh, and thanks for helping get the reports out the other day." Peter handed her several pages of handwritten proposal copy.

Sarah sat back at her desk, opened up Microsoft PowerPoint, and typed in the words of the proposal as Peter had scrawled them down. She went methodically through the verbiage, and added graphics as needed.

She'd worked about twenty minutes when Peter called her. "Hey there. I'm sorry to spring this on you, but we need to pick up a commercial from one of our agencies. It's one of Tina's accounts, but she's in another pitch right now, and this commercial starts airing later today."

Sarah was perturbed. "You know I'm working on this thing you want for next week."

"Yeah, I know. It can wait til you get back with the commercial. This is a new client, and they're running a promotion that starts this weekend, so they need the ad on now."

Sarah said, "All right," and hung up the phone. She locked her computer, and grabbed her purse. She knew the commercial was important -- the station would lose money if it didn't air on time -- but the fact Peter expected that she dropped everything without any consideration of her schedule annoyed her to no end.

Sarah had worked at the radio station for several months, and knew the local business partners and where she needed to go. She arrived at the agency office, and found the disc at the front with the receptionist. She flew back to WZEB, handed the commercial to the production manager, and returned to her cubicle to find Rhonda and Ted, the busiest and nastiest of the salespeople hovered near her desk. They held papers in their hands that Sarah assumed were account claim forms.

Another of Sarah's responsibilities was the claims for accounts. The salespeople were allowed a limited number of businesses on their list of accounts. Any account they wanted had to be requested by an account claim form sent to Sarah, who then updated the master list. If two or more people claimed an account, the matter went to Peter.

"What's going on?" Sarah asked cautiously.

Ted spoke first. "Sarah, I need you to put in this claim for Blazier Mattress. They're opening this week, and I plan..."

Rhonda interrupted. "No way. Sarah, don't do it. Ted, that's mine. You can't have it."

"Don't be stupid," Ted replied, turning back to Sarah, "Put it on my list."

"Go back to your car and bar accounts, and leave this one alone," Rhonda quipped.

"No, I don't think so," Ted countered. "Just because you're neighbors with the owner doesn't mean you can steal the account."

Sarah rolled her eyes. Two adults, in age anyway. It was like two dogs that fought over a bone. She grabbed both claim forms and said, "Look, you know how it works. These go to Peter to decide. Leave me out of this."

They both were taken aback by Sarah's quick response. Giving her a nasty look, Ted said, "That one better be mine." He strode off. Sarah retorted, "See how far that gets you next time you need my help."

Rhonda was slightly more diplomatic. She pleaded, "Come on, honey. Help me out here. I need to make my sales quota this month, or I'm in trouble."

Sarah felt sorry for Rhonda, but knew if she didn't follow the rules what that meant for her as Sarah. "Sorry, Rhonda, you have to take this up with Peter." Rhonda shook her head, and walked off. Sarah could relate to someone trying to make ends meet. While her situation in life brought her a lot of worry, it also helped make her a strong-willed person.

Sarah took another look at the draft of Peter's proposal. She had considered going into sales from time to time. Peter mentioned it periodically, and the potential for more money was hard to pass up. However, when she saw people like Ted and Rhonda: clawing and kicking even more than she already was, it stopped her from a switch. No matter how bad things were, she just felt it wasn't worth it. She took a lot of pride in being real with herself and with others. That was another reason she couldn't be in sales. She saw what even good salespeople did at times: kowtowed to clients, fudged facts, sneaked accounts from one another. She couldn't accept it if she lowered herself.

First and foremost, she supported her sons. Tough as it got at times, her mom's offers of assistance were something she didn't want. It wasn't the offers that bothered her, but the knowledge of her mom's situation added to her guilt that she asked in the first place.

Still, the anxiety over her financial situation was palpable, and she figured it wouldn't hurt to at least touch base with her mom. Besides, it had been a stressful day, and a friendly voice was always a nice thing.

She picked up her office phone. The line rang several times

before Louise answered. "Hi, Mom," Sarah replied half-heartedly.

"Well hello, sweetheart? How's my baby doing?" Louise said.

"Okay, I guess."

"You sure?"

"No, not really." Sarah felt tightness in her stomach and her throat. Her eyes teared up slightly. "Mama, I'm having trouble."

In a concerned and hushed tone, Louise said, "What's the matter?"

Sarah took a deep breath. "It's just everything, Mama: my life, the bills, not having enough time. I'm starting to fall behind on this credit card of mine, and my savings are almost gone. The boys need new clothes; their jeans are starting to get frayed. I bought some clothes from Goodwill, but they need better ones. I'm just worried I'm not gonna make it, Mama. I'm scared."

As Sarah spoke, her voice wavered. She glanced reflexively out of her cubicle to see if anyone was in earshot. The last thing she wanted was someone at work who heard her this emotional. No, the coast was clear. A tear rolled down her cheek. "They've been acting up in school again, too. I just don't know what I'm doing anymore." She sniffed.

Louise sighed. Her voice broke slightly as she replied, "My poor, sweet baby. I know you're going through a lot. Why don't I get the boys some clothes? I'm sure I can at least help you out there. I'm so sorry you're feeling like this."

Sarah quickly brushed another tear aside. Her voice quivered slightly as she replied, "I know. I really don't want to come to you with this, Mom. You have enough to worry about on your own without my stuff."

Like Sarah, Louise had a fairly rocky road in life. Abandoned by her husband at a young age, she raised Sarah and Kelly on her own. Louise provided with little funds a lot of the time. She'd often worked two jobs, and cut corners wherever possible, so she made ends meet. Sarah always admired her tenacity.

Louise cut Sarah off, "Now look. You're my little girl. Don't you forget that. You can come to me with any problem, and I'll help you any way I can. Don't you ever think you can't come to me. You're my life, Sarah, and I love you. Okay, baby?"

Sarah squeezed her eyes shut, and sobbed softly. Her mom's

71

words came through the phone like a hug. "Thank you, Mom, I love you too." She sighed, and tried to collect her self composure. It was still early in the day, when most salespeople were out of the office, and she hoped that Peter wasn't nearby for any of this.

"Sarah," Louise said, "I've told you this before, but I'll say it again. You're a strong woman. You've always been strong. You know, some people wouldn't have attempted to raise two boys on their own, and you started on that path when you were in your teens. I'm proud of you, baby. I just wish you'd realize that sometimes we need help from other people to make it in this world."

Sarah said, "I feel like I need to make up for the mistakes I've made."

Louise replied, "Mistakes? Sarah, you think you're the only one who makes mistakes?"

"Seems like it at times."

"In life, sometimes you stumble, sometimes you fall. But you get back up, dust yourself off and keep going. That's the way you succeed."

"Yeah, mom. But I think of Kelly. She never seems to need help. She's up there in New York, doing her thing. Why do things always work out for her?"

"Oh honey, don't think for a minute that Kelly doesn't have her own problems to deal with. She's living in a tiny one bedroom apartment, and can't afford to do anything but go to class. If it weren't for her financial aid, she wouldn't be able to afford that school at all."

Sarah smiled, and said, "Thanks, Mom. I needed that. Sorry I haven't been around to visit lately."

Louise said, "That's alright, baby."

"We'll make time soon."

"Good enough. Just keep your head up, and stay positive. Your babies need you, and so do I."

Sarah replied, "Okay, Mom. I'll try. You always made it look so easy, though."

"Oh I had my tough times, baby. Believe me. I was just able to hide it from you and Kelly fairly well."

"Thanks again, I love you! Talk with you later!"

Sarah hung up the phone. She sighed. She felt better about her situation for the time being. Her mom always had a way that cheered her up when she most needed it.

Sarah felt a second wind and went back to Peter's sales proposal.

Chapter Ten

As time passed, Michael went on the Facebook page for *Stewardesses* more and more. It picked up his gloomy mood, for the most part anyway.

The Save *Stewardesses* movement was in full swing, and several petitions had been created, for those who wanted a place where they expressed their interest in the series on the web. The E! Online website had even added *Stewardesses* to their annual listing of "Vote To Keep The Shows" poll.

Michael woke around 8, and checked Twitter to see if anything new was there. Instead, he saw a tweet from Charlotte.

@CharloteDucrest We have received "The call", after holiday break we are back for one more episode! TYVM for your support! #Stewardesses

Michael stared at his phone for a moment. Was that really it? They pulled the plug on the series, even before they finished one season? Had anyone at the TV network noticed all the buzz *Stewardesses* got on Facebook, Twitter and the rest of the internet? He planned on looking into this in more detail when he had more time.

He checked the time, and shut off his computer. Time for his job interview with Quicksolve.

Michael sported a blazer and slacks. With a red tie and his jacket buttoned, he was dressed to go.

The reception area at Quicksolve was sleek and modern. The front entrance was mostly glass, with the company logo frosted on the main door. The small, curved reception desk was set back several feet from the door. The wall behind the reception desk curved a bit, and held a single door. There was a waiting area to the far right with a small table and four plush chairs.

When Michael arrived, he asked the receptionist to call Jack. He walked over to the waiting area, and sank slowly into one of the chairs. He fidgeted with his tie, and a short time later Jack walked through the door by the receptionist desk. He glanced over at Michael, beamed and walked up to him. Jack reached out his hand, and said, "Wow you're almost respectable!"

Michael smirked and replied, "Thanks... please don't laugh too hard at the clothes."

"I'll try."

"Feels a little strange being dressed up and not going to a wedding or funeral."

"That's the professional world."

"So how does this work?"

"Christine from human resources will bring you back for the interview. Takes around fifteen to twenty minutes usually. Mine went about thirty, but I had more experience to talk about."

"What's it like?"

"She'll look over your resume, ask you about it. She may also ask stuff like where you want to be in five years."

"In five years? I don't know where I want to be in five months!"

"Just say something positive, like you want to be a network administrator."

Michael looked around the reception area. The receptionist glanced down at her desk at the moment. He sat down in his chair, scratched the back of his head and sighed. "Okay then, let's do this."

Jack nodded. "Good luck. You'll be great. Just be natural."

"Yeah, I'll try. Hope they take a chance on me."

"We won't know until you try."

"Yep."

"We'll get you gainfully employed. No more price checks or some shit." Jack grinned.

Michael squinted slightly. "Ouch. Well maybe I can get this or something else soon."

Jack placed his hands on Michael's shoulders. "Catch up with you tonight."

"That'll work."

"Ales?"

Michael nodded. Jack left, and Michael sat back in the chair. He saw several magazines on a nearby table. He picked up a technology magazine, flipped through the pages, gazed at the ads, and any headlines that caught his attention. He thought about where he wanted to be in five years. Several ideas sprang to mind, but probably none that made a desirable answer in a job interview. He imagined being a cast member on a TV series like *Stewardesses*. Yeah, that would be interesting. He imagined himself a part of the entertainment business, trips to the Emmys, things like that.

The door Jack had disappeared through opened again, and Christine stepped into the reception area. She focused her gaze on Michael for a moment, smiled and strode toward him. Her appearance and body language was confident and professional. Her somewhat large frame was not off-putting, but he could tell she was someone who commanded a room. She was dressed conservatively, with wire-rimmed glasses and curly blonde hair that cascaded down past her shoulders.

"You must be Jack's friend, Michael. I'm Christine. Welcome to Quicksolve." She extended her hand.

Michael stood up, shook her hand, and replied, "It's great to meet you. So how do we get started?"

"Let's head back to the conference room. We'll have a little chat, and that should be fine for today."

Michael nodded and said, "I'm all yours."

Christine led Michael into a moderately sized room that

continued the general design of the reception area, but without all the glass. Pieces of decorative wood trim were evenly spaced around the ceiling, giving the sleekness of the office a slight touch of classic sophistication.

Christine motioned Michael to a chair, then seated herself on the other side of the table. There was a file folder with several documents on the table in front of her. She retrieved one that looked like his resume.

"So," she began, "Tell me about what you've done in the way of technical support."

Michael tried not to fidget, though he was not comfortable in his outfit. "Well, um, I've been online a lot, and I've been pretty active with people on websites like Facebook and Twitter. I know that may not seem like much, but I've been someone that people can go to when they have problems doing things online."

Christine jotted notes on a pad, nodding. "Can you be more specific?"

"Well, I follow a Facebook group for a TV series called *Stewardesses*, you may have heard of it. The group has online polls and quizzes, and sometimes people have trouble accessing parts of the group."

"And you help them out?"

"Lot of the time, yeah. Maybe it's a problem with their web browser, maybe it's just that they aren't very computer savvy. I've been able to help several people out there with using the Facebook group as they need."

Christine smiled. "Ahh, I see. That's interesting. And yes, I'm familiar with *Stewardesses*. Great show, hope they get another season."

Michael's eyebrows rose slightly. He had a sudden surge of confidence. She was a fan, they had a connection. That had to be good, right? "Hey, yeah I agree. It's so nice to meet a fellow fan." He smiled.

"Of course. I've been around on Twitter, too, during the episodes. Lot of fun."

"No kidding. I'm on there as @Tim707."

Christine stared at him for a few moments, before she managed a slight chuckle. "Well, looks like we've already met. I'm

77

@FlirtyMonique."

Michael laughed and nodded. This had to be a good omen.

She gazed over his resume. "Well, looks like you don't have a whole lot of direct technical support experience."

Michael sunk a little into his chair.

She looked up at him, and continued, "The fact that you help people on Facebook as you described isn't bad. Of course, we prefer people with job experience directly related to what we do here, but taking your own initiative as you've done on Facebook counts for something. Now, we monitor what our employees do on the web here, so if we hire you, you'd of course be expected to stay away from those sites during business hours, unless it's directly related to work." She adjusted her glasses.

Michael nodded. "Right. I usually just jump on during work breaks. I'll be careful."

After Christine scanned his resume a few more moments, she added, "I don't know how much Jack told you about this position, but it's for a Technical Support Analyst."

"Not much, but I gather it's a lot of phone calls?"

"Yes, you'll be on a phone most of your day, responding to any number of issues our customers have. Are you familiar with our travel website?"

"Not directly, I'm afraid. The bulk of my travel to date is to places you can drive to in less than six hours."

She frowned slightly. "Well, I advise you take a look at the website to get familiar with it, if we decide to move forward with you on anything."

As Michael continued to answer questions, Christine made notes on a pad. He guessed it was part of being sized up. The whole thing was worlds different from what he'd done before. When he got the job at B&G, he just filled out the application, and said when he could start. They cared little to none about his goals, and sure as hell not about any resume.

She checked over Michael's resume and her own written notes for a few more minutes before she looked back up at him. She set the papers down on the desk, lowered her glasses slightly, and peered at him over the frames. "Tell me, Michael, what's your greatest weakness?"

Michael sat for a minute, and blinked. *My greatest weakness?* he thought.

Women in 1960s Stewardess outfits?

Sarah's face when she laughs at one of my jokes?

The need to make my parents see me as my own man?

His brow furrowed in thought, he sat back in his chair for a moment, glanced up towards the ceiling, and breathed deeply. Christine gazed at him. "Come on now, I'm not your therapist. I don't need your dirt. But there must be something," she chuckled softly.

He moved his gaze from the ceiling back to her, and said, "I have a hard time asking for help. That's my weakness."

Christine pondered his response, and jotted down a few more notes on her pad. As she wrote, she commented, "That's actually not the first time I've heard that in an interview. Care to elaborate?"

"Well, I'm a guy who likes to figure things out for himself. The things I have done with computers, so far I've mostly figured out on my own. I Google answers to problems. Maybe that's 'asking for help', but I make a point to not directly ask people as much as possible."

Christine nodded. "I see. That's not necessarily a bad thing, but sometimes getting another opinion or perspective solves a problem faster."

"Yeah, I see your point. Asking other people directly is not my first approach though."

She looked through the rest of her notes and said, "Well, Michael, I think that about wraps this up. Thanks for coming in today. We'll let you know if we need you." She got up from the desk, and gestured to the door. Michael followed her, and once they had returned to the reception area, he thanked her, and left the building.

Back in his car, Michael felt his tension rapidly subside. With the windows up, he let out a yell. All in all, he felt good. Not only did he have a resume, but he went on his first real job interview. Something was about to happen for him. He just wished it would, already.

Chapter Eleven

Ales was slow that night. It was late October, and high school football season was almost over. Since it was a Friday and game night, a fair amount of Ales regulars focused on their kids social activities, games, and other events.

There were only three customers besides Michael at the bar, and five tables were filled. Sarah was there, as she covered for a bartender who was sick. Michael sat comfortably on a barstool, happy about how his interview went. He set his beer on the bar to ask Sarah how she was doing.

"Oh, just wonderful."

"Any freebies lately, t-shirts, movie passes?"

"Not much there. I'm just dealing with my boss and keeping salespeople from ripping each other's heads off."

"Oh fun."

"It's a joyride. The station's doing some live broadcasts this weekend so I may come out, grab a little free food."

"Hey, I may have to join you there."

"Go for it, I take the perks when I can!"

Michael nodded. "I can definitely relate."

"When you have three mouths to feed including your own, sometimes you gotta stretch the budget." Sarah noticed Michael was smiling and asked, "What'd you do today? And what's with the goofy-ass grin?"

Michael leaned back on his barstool, and said proudly, "Job interview!"

Sarah's expression changed to surprise. "Wow, good for you! Where?"

"Jack's work. They're looking for tech support people."

"That's great!"

"I guess. Took some work, but I got a resume together for them."

Sarah mused and replied, "Yeah, those can be a bitch. The temp agency I work at helped me out with mine."

Michael said, "The interview was interesting. It was just me in a room with the HR person, and we talked for a while."

"How did it go?"

"She told me about the kind of worker they were looking to hire, asked about what I knew."

Sarah replied, "Yeah, that's pretty typical. You haven't been on a lot of interviews, have you?"

"No, I've pretty much just filled out applications and answered scheduling questions."

"So kind of like what I did here. The bartender world isn't much on job interviews. It's pretty much, 'Have you tended bar before?' 'For how long and where?' and 'Can you work weeknights and weekends?'"

"One thing I bet wasn't typical, we talked about *Stewardesses*."

"Really? You brought that up? Can't you stop talking about that, even for a job interview?"

"Hey, it came up!"

"Because you mentioned it."

Michael shrugged. "Turns out she's a fan too. I told her about helping people on the Facebook group, and how that was kinda like technical support."

"Uh huh. Well I'll be. Who knew your love of 60's airline stewardesses would be resume material?"

Michael finished his beer. When Sarah grabbed his glass to

refill it, Michael asked, "Speaking of *Stewardesses*, you check the Facebook group lately?"

Sarah handed him another beer and said, "When I can. Things have been up and down, so I haven't had time for that. Just checking email and a Facebook message here and there."

Michael replied, "Charlotte just tweeted today. Looks like they're gonna be pulling the series soon."

"No! So that's it?"

Michael shrugged, and studied his glass. "The Save *Stewardesses* movement is still rolling. People are posting fan videos left and right."

"Oh yeah?"

"Yeah, pretty much. There's several up on YouTube already. Of course, the folks who're into the Tim and Monique romance have a lot to look through."

"Aww, nice. Can't say they don't have the backing."

"Yep. Just hope the network folks see all this, and think twice about canceling."

"I wonder how much the actors are taking part in this Save *Stewardesses* thing."

"Oh, I can tell you for sure Charlotte's on the Facebook group page. She replied to a message of mine recently."

Sarah smiled. "Oh, yeah, you mentioned that."

"We'll see."

"Hey, maybe things are starting to turn around a bit."

Michael smiled. The email from his dad popped into his mind. Even though he'd deleted it, and was proud that he had, it still gnawed at him. He thought, *Maybe I need another perspective. Sarah would be a good person to ask about this. We always talked with each other about personal stuff and family things. Maybe she'd have some advice for this situation.*

Sarah had gone to the other end of the bar to get a customer a beer. Michael called out to her, "Hey Sarah, need to ask you something, when you have a sec." She waved back in reply.

While Michael waited for Sarah to return, he heard Jack's voice coming from behind him. "Did you kill it?"

Turning around, Michael held up his hands to high-five Jack. Smiling, he said, "Like a pro, man. Like a pro."

"That's what I like to hear!"

"Guess we'll see what happens, right? Any inside information for me?"

"I know they liked you, but not much else. She ask any unusual questions?"

"Well she didn't ask me that five year question, but she asked me about my biggest weakness."

"Ahh, yeah that's another one. What'd you tell her, the series *Stewardesses*?"

"Shut up. I gave her a real answer."

"And that was...?"

"I'm not gonna tell you everything, dude!" Michael laughed, and turned back to the bar. Jack sat down on the barstool next to Michael. Sarah returned to stand near them and said, "Well, if it isn't my two favorite drunks? What can I get you, Jack?"

Jack scanned the row of taps behind Sarah. He looked back at her and said, "Let's try a Guinness this time."

Sarah, with a shocked face, turned to the taps. Michael said, "Well, at least they liked me. That's got to help, right?"

Jack nodded quickly, "Definitely."

"She apparently likes *Stewardesses* anyway, so we talked a little about that."

"Or you brought it up?" Jack chuckled.

"What is it with you two tonight?"

Jack slapped his shoulder, "Relax man, messing with ya."

"I figured being liked there would be good."

"Of course."

Sarah returned with the Guinness. Jack and Michael toasted the interview. After they finished, Sarah asked, "Michael, you wanted to say something?"

Michael put his glass on the bar. Looking at Sarah, he thought, *Should I bring this up with Jack here? I guess, since I'm not going to stop thinking about it until I deal with it.*

Michael said, "Well, you both know my situation with my parents. I haven't had much contact with them other than seeing them out at a restaurant."

Jack sipped his beer as Sarah wiped the bar.

"Today I got an email from my dad. I thought about replying, but I wasn't really sure how, so I just deleted it."

Sarah slapped her hands on the bar and regarded Michael. "You deleted it? Why? What did it say?"

"Oh, he asked how I was, and to let him know."

Sarah stared at him for a moment. "So your father, whom you haven't spoken with much at all... way less than you used to, asks you how you're doing, and you just brush him off like he's bothering you?"

"Uh, I guess so." Michael shifted a bit on the barstool. He glanced at Jack, who looked equally incredulous as Sarah.

Feeling doubtful, Michael glanced back at Sarah. She grabbed a rag, and wiped the bar down furiously for a few moments, in thought over Michael's latest move. She stopped, and glanced up at him, saying, "Well, what's so bad about letting your dad know how you are, Michael? He's trying to reach out."

"Yeah, well, I did talk with them at the restaurant a little."

"So what's the big deal? Believe me, if I didn't see either of my boys for a few days, I'd be worried sick."

"Hey, let's not forget why I was out of there in the first place."

"Yeah, your parents kicked you out, but you needed a push," Jack added.

Michael sighed, "Well."

"Well nothing, you broke a deal! Are you really that selfish, ignoring a simple email?" Sarah gasped.

Michael shrugged and replied, "I don't know, guess I'm not ready. It just seemed that no matter what I did, it was never good enough, and I'm trying to get something going first before I get back into talking with them again."

"You have the limo business now, and you have this interview," Jack said.

Michael replied, "Yeah, but is it enough? Otherwise it's just a matter of time before I'm doing something else they don't like."

Sarah asked, "Have you considered your father may still care how you're doing? I'm sure they didn't want to cut off contact for good."

"I'm just not ready yet. I need more time."

Sarah threw up her hands, exasperated. She left to collect the empty glasses on the bar. Jack said, "Michael, dude, you can't keep doing this. It works both ways."

Michael thought about their reaction. The truth was, he didn't have a good reason to delete the email, or avoid contact with his parents. For the first time, he saw his actions about it as childish. "All right," he said. "Maybe I'll give them a call."

Jack slapped the bar. "Excellent idea. You can tell yourself they gave in first, if it's that important."

Michael winced slightly at Jack's sarcasm. It stung, but there was a good deal of truth behind his words. Sarah returned, her arms folded. She looked at Jack and asked, "Have you talked some sense into him yet?"

Jack replied, "Yeah, I think he's fine."

Sarah said, "Good. Really, Michael. Sometimes you need a good smack in the head."

Michael leaned forward, arched an eyebrow, and replied, "Oh really? You offering?"

Sarah popped the top of Michael's head in a moderate slap. Michael quickly fell back on his barstool, and laughed. "Ow. Alright, you two. I get your point."

Sarah smiled. She was glad she had Michael and Jack to fool around with as a break from her worries. There would always be bills, hassles with her sons' schedules, things to put up with at the radio station, but she knew she had two guys that she looked to as a haven.

Jack asked Sarah, "So when are we getting Foo Fighter tickets from you?"

Sarah cocked her head, and retorted, "Uh, get in line, buddy. Those tickets, if I ever see any, are mine."

"What about some MP3s or a shirt or anything?" Michael pleaded.

Sarah snapped her fingers. "Heel, boy. Besides, Ales has live music starting in a few weeks. That should be enough to satisfy your cravings for goodies."

"I'll come to a few shows," Jack replied. "How about you, Michael?"

"Sure, might as well." He turned to Sarah, and asked, "What kind of bands are they getting?"

Sarah pulled out a flyer from behind the bar. Studying it, she said, "Looks like local acts only. Guess I'll have to wait to see Mr. Grohl at a different venue."

Michael and Jack laughed.

Jack said, "Well, I hate to cut this short, but it is a 'school night,' and I need to get me some rest." His hand on Michael's shoulder, he said, "Glad it went well. If I hear anything, I'll let you know. Heading out now?"

Michael nodded, and said, "Yeah I guess so." Turning to Sarah, he said, "Good night, dear! See you soon!"

"Bye, guys!" Sarah said, as she picked up their empty glasses, and watched them walk out of Ales.

Chapter Twelve

Sarah busied herself behind the bar, straightened bottles, and took out the trash. It was a lighter night as far as tips went, but that was just the way it was sometimes. She patted her hips in thought, and moved around to the front of the bar by the stools.

Then she saw something on the floor. The lights were up, but no matter how she tried, she never made out what it was at first. Maybe her vision was a little hazy from just hard work. It was a small case or something. A phone, maybe?

No, it was a wallet.

She looked around. A few people cleaned in the kitchen and the back, but no one was up there with her. She thought about the lost and found box, then she stopped.

Her hand massaged the leather. It felt kind of thick. She pushed away the thoughts popping into her head for a few moments, but curiosity got the better of her, and she opened it.

The bills inside fanned out, and taunted her. *So much money here. Wonder if this belongs to that lawyer guy who stared at my tits all night and talked about how nice it looked when I reached over for something?*

She set the wallet on the bar, and continued her work. The thoughts continued... the guy hadn't tipped her much, either. Maybe two or three dollars on the five whiskey sours he had? He'd be lucky if his ass didn't get pulled over. DWI and no license? Real nice.

She reached the far end of the barstool area. Her eyes focused on the wallet as she walked back. *All those bills. What if I just took a few? I saw a fifty in there. Maybe just a twenty? He was loaded off his ass, would he know it was missing?*

Her thoughts went to her credit cards and other bills. *How much can Mom help me, after all? I'm just getting by. Why not just a little extra here. He just about ignored my tip. Why the hell am I working these hours away from my boys if I'm not making decent money? How else am I supposed to catch up on bills?*

If Jimmy was with her, she knew what he'd say. *"Take it all. Dumb ass shouldn't be so careless. Serves 'em right."* He'd even run up the credit cards if he could.

No, too easy to track that. But just a few dollars more?

She peered into the wallet one more time.

Chapter Thirteen

Michael stretched his arms out over his head and yawned. He was two hours into his Wednesday shift at B&G, and boredom settled over him right on schedule. It didn't help that it was mid afternoon, when only a slow stream of customers meandered in the store, and he had long periods of nothing to do.

He wondered about his Quicksolve interview last week. He figured he had at least another week to wait before he heard anything, but he still wondered about his chances. Jack seemed to think it had gone well, but, then again, Jack was always an optimist. Michael wondered if he, Michael, a college dropout with a series of dead-end jobs, was ready for a corporate career. He wondered if the words "Michael" and "career" belonged in the same sentence. All he knew up until now were "jobs", working 8, 9 or 10 hours a day at a bar, restaurant, or grocery store until he either pissed off his boss and got fired, or a better job came along and he took it.

To Michael, the concept of someone who had a regular series of the same type of work, and built a retirement and so on overwhelmed him a bit. It just seemed so involved. He knew his parents had done it, and they certainly seemed to be comfortable in their house. Their house, he thought to himself. Up until recently it felt more like it was part his house too.

Michael took out his smartphone, and checked his email. Nothing from Quicksolve was in his inbox. He checked to see if his spam filter had caught it, but it wasn't in the junk box either. *I don't want to seem too anxious and call them the very next day,* he thought to himself. *It would be better to hold off for now.*

He thought about his parents, and his conversation with Sarah and Jack about them. *Maybe I am being childish here,* he thought to himself. *Dad has always tried to make me be my own person, and maybe throwing me on my ass is the only way he had left to do it. I should call them. No, it's during work. I should speak with them in private in case things get heated again.*

While he stared at his phone, someone asked him, "Are you open?" He looked up, and saw a middle-aged man who held a package of paper towels and some packs of coffee. Michael quickly put his phone away, and began to total up the man's order. While Michael entered the items into his register, the man said, "So, you're into those smartphones, huh?"

Michael glanced up quickly. "What? Oh, yeah. They're great. Can't believe we all used to use computers for a lot of this stuff." Before he returned his gaze to his register, Michael noticed a logo on the man's shirt: Tech 4 U, which was the technology store in town at the Lakeside Shopping Center. The man was heavyset around the waist but Michael was able to spy a new smart phone in a holster on his belt. He appeared to walk the walk with being into the latest gear, at least on his phone.

The man replied, "Yeah really. Sounds like you're really into that stuff."

"Yep," Michael smiled as he swiped groceries across the scanner.

"I own Tech 4 U, and I'm looking for people who're into technology and can explain it to my customers. You know, show them laptops, smart phones and gadgets and give advice on the best ones to buy."

Michael ignored his register and the groceries for a moment. "I've been to Tech 4 U a few times. Lot of neat things on display there."

"Ha, well gotta grab people walking by."

"I first saw the smart phone I ended up with now on display there."

"I see. Yeah, we sell a lot of those phones. We're also an AT&T service provider, so that helps."

"Oh, didn't realize that."

"You know, I bet you'd do pretty well working in a store like mine."

A big smile found its way to Michael's face, as he tried to keep focused on things. Doing that was tougher in this case, for some reason. "That'll be $26.72."

The man handed him a credit card. As Michael processed the payment, the man leaned closer to Michael, and in a hushed voice said, "Hey, I don't mean to pry, but I bet you aren't making a lot of money here, and the work isn't that interesting."

Michael glanced around. "Can't say I'd miss it."

"If you want, stop by and let me show you around."

A rush of energy burst through Michael. He tried to keep his chuckle stifled, and just nodded fast. "Yeah. I'll do that."

The man smiled in response. "Good, I think you'd be great at it." As Michael handed him his receipt and credit card, the man passed Michael his business card.

The man said, "My name's Kenny."

Michael replied, "Hi, Kenny. I'm-

"-Michael." Kenny said, then grinned, and pointed to the nametag. Michael smiled back.

They shook hands, and Kenny left. It didn't seem real to Michael at first. *A job offer in the checkout line? Was this how Jack got into IT? No, couldn't have been that simple. He had the college degree, and went through interviews like I had at Quicksolve. This guy sure seemed legit, and the electronics plus smartphone sales would sure as hell beat what he did here.*

He watched as Kenny drove off, then Ms. Rose blurted out, "Hey, Michael." He turned to see her in his checkout line.

"Hi."

"Don't expect you've spoken with Brad in the past day or two?"

"Not so much, he's been working late."

She shook her head. "The rent was due three days ago. I've been trying to call him, but he hasn't answered. You and he need to have that money to me by tomorrow evening."

"I'm sorry, I didn't know, I gave him my half-"

"Just get it to me, okay?" She nodded, and walked off.

Great. For someone who lived with him, he didn't see Brad much. Of course, Michael also hardly checked on Brad most of the time anyway, as he was usually in a bad mood, had a hangover or both.

He called Brad on the way to his lunch break. Of course, it went to voicemail.

"Hey Brad - Ms. Rose said she needs the rent money tomorrow night. I left my half on the counter by the coffee maker, alright? Call me back when you get this."

***

Michael sat in the B&G employee break room, ate a roast beef sandwich from the B&G deli, and drank some water. He thought of how options had appeared all of a sudden. The more he thought about a job in technology the more he thought it would be a good fit for him.

He'd never thought he'd get a job offer in his checkout line, though. Work in electronics was new to him, but he was pretty adept at using his phone and laptop already, and besides he already made a leap with the Quicksolve interview. Why rule out anyone else?

Tech 4 U was a proud local standout that sold electronics amid the many big box stores like Best Buy, the Apple Store and the like. They hung on as of late, because people in New Orleans were supportive of local businesses, and that was enough for the store's survival for now. Michael had been to Tech 4 U on several occasions, so he knew it fairly well. It was definitely the kind of work Michael preferred.

Michael gulped some water as his phone rang. He checked the caller ID, and saw it was Quicksolve.

"Hello?"

"Hello, Michael. This is Christine from Quicksolve."

"Hi."

"I wanted to thank you for coming into our office last week for the interview. Unfortunately, we decided to choose someone else for this position."

"Oh, I see. Didn't think you'd call to tell me no."

"Well, I know you're Jack's friend, so I thought I'd keep you from wondering."

"Ah, thanks."

"I'm sorry. We'll keep your resume on file for further job openings though, okay?"

Michael replied, "Yeah, thanks for letting me know." He ended the call. So much for that option, he thought. It sure seemed kind of quick. Oh well.

With Quicksolve off the table, Michael thought more about Kenny from Tech 4 U. He seemed very interested in Michael. Michael figured since he now had nothing to lose, he made Tech 4 U his first stop after he left B&G that day.

***

Kenny was way more than just talk. In about thirty minutes, Michael went from a tour of Tech 4 U to a job offer, with a decent bump in pay. He felt a surge of optimism as he strolled out of the mall, and figured out when his last day at B&G would be.

His phone rang again. Not checking the caller ID, he answered, "So, Jack... you couldn't have given me the heads-up I was wasting my time?"

Michael heard his dad's voice on the other end. "Uh, Michael?"

Michael froze. He hadn't heard his dad's voice in a few weeks. He struggled with a response, and simply managed a, "Hi Dad."

His father continued. "How are you?"

"I'm alright." Michael wanted to add how he was fine without them, but it never came out. He remembered what Sarah and Jack had told him, this was his parent, and his intention had nothing to do with spite or hatred.

Michael's father said, "That's good. Listen, I'm calling about your mother. She's in Ochsner Hospital."

"What happened?"

"Bacterial infection in her bloodstream."

"Oh no, how bad?"

"It's touch and go right now. She's in the I... ICU."

As John explained the situation, and his voice cracked, Michael felt a burning knot in his stomach. The possibility of a loss either parent was something he never wanted to consider, at least not at this point.

Michael's voice broke as he said, "Dad, I'd like to see her, if that's okay."

"Of course, son. You never have to ask that."

"Okay, I'll come by the house when I get off work today."

"Sounds good, Michael. See you then."

Michael ended the call, and bowed his head. His head spun at the turn of events. His anger over the situation with his parents quickly evolved into worry over the situation of his mother's condition. Why is this happening to her, he wondered. Barbara was a kind and loving person who generously gave of herself to many. She didn't deserve this.

After getting off work at B&G, Michael drove to his parent's house. He saw his father sitting on the sofa in the living room. His father looked at him and smiled, said, "Well hello, have a seat."

Michael walked up to his father, and held out his arms for a hug. The sight of Michael in this pose, and his expression of concern, brought his father to his feet, and they embraced.

"It's good to see you," John said.

"You too, Dad," replied Michael.

They sat down on the sofa. John said, "ICU visiting hours aren't for another hour and a half."

"So what's the plan for Mom?"

John leaned forward, and faced away from Michael. He placed his elbows on his knees, and clasped his hands together. His head tilted downward, he said, "All they can do for her now is administer antibiotics. They still say her chances are good, and I'm clinging on to that."

Michael faced John, and placed his hand on his father's shoulder. "Dad, how did this happen?"

"Well, as you know your mother has diabetes. They say that contributed to this. She came down with a virus not long after you

94

left. At first, she was just having some pains. Fever and her staying in bed came next. Then, she stopped eating, and we had to bring her in. It's quite possible she's had this infection for a while, but it really started to affect her a few weeks ago. Then it just kind of unraveled from there. Next thing I knew, they're telling me she has to go in the ICU."

Michael asked, "Is she conscious?"

"Somewhat. She drifts in and out. I've been visiting her several times since she went in."

"Is she eating?"

"Mostly via IV. A little by mouth when she's awake long enough."

"Can she talk at all?"

"Very little." John sighed, and added, "I read to her sometimes. Or I just talk about the day."

Michael smiled. He figured his father would be tending to her like that. His parents had a very caring relationship.

John settled back in his chair a bit, and asked, "So how did that car work out?"

"Well, radiator needed replacing. Hopefully that's the last repair for awhile."

"Ahh, well that's part of running a business, expenses."

"Yeah, well we're getting more dates booked."

"That's great! So what else have you been up to?"

He thought back to Sarah and Jack, and how they encouraged him for this. He sat up, smiled and said, "Well, you'd be proud of me, Dad. I've got a resume and already had one job interview."

John's eyebrows arched. "Resume? Interview?"

"Yep! It didn't go my way, but I have the resume now. And, I was offered a job today at Tech 4 U, as a technology consultant!"

John sat back on the couch, impressed. "Wow, that's great! I've been to Tech 4 U."

"Yeah, owner came right through my line at B&G, and I guess he liked what I had to say."

"It's a step in the right direction, son. I'm proud of you."

Michael heard the words from his father: "I'm proud of you." The words themselves felt like a hug. He knew that in the grand scheme of things, his job at Tech 4 U might not have lead to anything, but those simple words from his father were positively golden. His voice cracked as Michael managed a quick, "Thanks, Dad."

John asked, "So are you still hooked on that show... what was it, *Stewardesses*?"

Michael chuckled, "Oh you bet. My friends Jack and Sarah are also."

John laughed, "Dear lord, you've been recruiting."

"Guess so, well won't be much longer for that."

"Canceled?"

"Not yet, but it's in dire straits. There's a lot of buzz online about saving the show."

"Is that so? I'm betting you're mixing it up a bit there too on the internet?"

"Every week, with lots of other people."

"That amazes me, how much people are involved on the internet with things like that, a TV show. Back when I was younger, we just watched shows on TV and maybe talked about them afterward or the next day or so. Now, it seems like people are almost a part of the crew, the way they go on about it."

"Not too far off, dad. I'm still logging in on Twitter as a character from the show, and tweeting people."

John marveled, "You should've started a job with computers much sooner."

"Looks like I will be now, and I'm doing a lot on Facebook too."

"My son, the social networking giant."

Michael and his father laughed. The tension that existed since Michael's departure had cooled. Father and son drove to see Barbara in the ICU at Ochsner. After they checked in at the nurses' station, a charge nurse took them into her room. As they walked through the ICU area, the various machines made an odd symphony of sorts. Ventilators mechanically gasped and wheezed as they breathed for their respective patients. Heart monitors faithfully chirped, as the lives that they helped struggled.

Barbara was attached to numerous IV drips, and she was sedated fairly heavily. John and Michael approached her bedside. It looked like she was up. John caressed Barbara's face, as he said softly, "Hi honey, how you feeling today?"

Barbara smiled at the sound of his voice and feel of his touch. She said softly, "Hey love. Good to see you. Who's that with you?"

John glanced back to Michael, and motioned him to come closer. As Michael approached, John stepped back, and gave him room. When she saw her son, Barbara's eyes widened. A tear formed at the corner of one of her eyes. She spoke in a voice barely above a whisper, "Michael, is that you?"

Michael nodded, tears formed in his eyes as well. "Hey, Mom. Sorry I haven't been around. I love you, and I'm just - sorry."

As Michael cried softly, he leaned forward. With what strength she had, Barbara held up one arm, and pulled him gently toward her. "My baby. That's all right. I love you too. I'm... glad to see you, sweetheart."

As Michael and Barbara embraced, John stood over them, his hands on Michael's shoulders. After a few moments, Michael stood upright again. He wiped his tears, and asked, "How're you feeling?"

Barbara glanced at John then back at Michael. "Well, I'm sure I look dreadful to you, but I'm doing better. The doctors seem to think they've found the right antibiotic for me. I'm on the right track, I suppose."

John squeezed his son's shoulders, and breathed a deep sigh of relief. "That's great. That's just wonderful. You take it easy, and do everything they tell you, dear."

Barbara smiled. John added, "And in the spirit of good news, Michael has something to share as well."

Barbara's expression became quizzical. She said, "What is it, sweetheart?"

He glanced quickly over his shoulder, and then back toward her. "Well, uh, Mom... I've been doing some job hunting. I got together a resume, and went on an interview where Jack works."

Barbara lightly touched Michael's arm. "That's wonderful! How did it go?"

"Didn't get it," Michael shrugged. "But lucky me, I met the owner of Tech 4 U at the grocery store. He offered me a job, I start there in a few days!"

Barbara beamed. She said to both Michael and John, "You see? Good things happen if you persevere. You just need to work at it."

Michael nodded, while he avoided any cynical thoughts over her comment as best he could. He replied, "Yeah, that's right. Just hope I don't mess it up."

Barbara replied, "Now why would you say that? You've got to keep positive, baby."

"I'm trying, mom."

"Keep trying, I'm proud of you." At that moment, her breathing became a bit more labored, and she wheezed as she added, "Just give it your best."

John said, "I think we'd better let you rest. I'll come back tomorrow, and I'm sure Michael wouldn't mind coming by soon either." He glanced at Michael, and waited for an acknowledgment.

Michael nodded quickly, replying, "Absolutely. I need to finish up working at B&G and see what my schedule for my new job will be. As soon as I know I'll make some time to come by."

Barbara said, "Sounds wonderful. Until then." John leaned over, and kissed her on the lips. Michael hugged her, and they exited the room.

As they walked back to the parking lot, John turned to Michael. "How does she look to you?" Michael turned to look at his father, and saw his worried expression. Michael glanced at his father for a moment. He realized while his dad had probably heard the official word from the doctor and nurses about Barbara's condition, he wanted Michael, his son and someone who knew how Barbara looked in good health, to have given an honest opinion of how she really seemed to be.

"I've seen her looking better, Dad. She's been through a lot. Adding a bacterial infection to the diabetes is above and beyond."

"She was pretty agitated when they brought her in here, yelling and hollering."

"Oh damn."

"Just glad that passed."

"She's taken care of herself over the years, and I can't imagine many diabetics take better care of themselves than her."

"You're right about that."

"This is just one more hurdle for her, but given the way she handles her health I think she's holding up well, considering."

John contemplated Michael's assessment, and glanced downward for a moment. He furrowed his brow, and looked directly at Michael. "What was that 'messing up at your job' about?"

"Aw, Dad. Are we going to do this now?"

"Well?"

"I have some fear of the unknown, you know. There's no guarantees what's gonna happen, and I don't want to disappoint you two."

John grabbed Michael's shoulder. "Son, nothing in life is certain. Well, very few things are certain. You're born, you die, and you spend a lot of time in between trying to figure things out. Those are the certainties in life. The rest of it is a series of risks. Every single day, there's another set of risks each of us face. You took a risk when you created a resume, and went on that job interview. Sure, it didn't pan out, but where would you have been if you hadn't tried that? Still where you were before. You took another risk in talking with the owner of Tech 4 U, and look how that one paid off. You've got to realize sometimes you'll win, sometimes you'll lose."

Michael nodded, and held his father's gaze. "Dad, I know. Sometimes it's like I'm not allowed to be concerned about what happens tomorrow. You always come back with some motivational comments and--while I do appreciate them--I feel like I'm not allowed to express my fears."

John replied, "I'm just trying to keep your mind on the things that matter."

Michael looked away. John grabbed him by the shoulder, their eyes met again. "You're my son, Michael. I love you, and I want this to work out for you. I just hope one day you realize that."

Michael said, "I'm trying, Dad. I love you too."

They embraced.

***

Once they returned to the house, Michael said goodbye to John, and drove back to his apartment. While Michael wanted the lifestyle he had now, he was happy that he now felt comfortable at his parents' house. Thanks to everyone, he came to realize how petty and needless his avoidance of his parents was.

On the ride back, he gave Sarah a call about his mom's situation. The phone rang for a few times before he heard the hollers of young voices. Not long after that, he heard a distinctly perturbed Sarah as she yelled, "Quiet NOW, or you're gonna get spanked til you can't sit down!" With that, the rabble quieted down, and Michael then heard Sarah say, "Hello?"

"How are ya?"

"Argh. Between homework and feeding these two, I feel like I'm in a prison camp. I'll survive. If I can make it through, how hard can the rest be, right?"

Michael laughed. "Good point. How's radio?"

"About the same. Been teaching new salespeople the ropes."

"Babysitting people who make more money than you?"

"Hey, that's the way it is."

"It's a living, right?

"Yeah. I'm amazed how many of them never worked on a computer aside from hitting the web. I don't mind helping them a little, but damn it if I'm going to set up their email contacts and crap like that. I might be an administrative assistant, but I'm nobody's bitch."

Michael said, "Sounds like they could use a tech support person over there."

"Sure would make MY life easier. But no, WZEB is all about doing it cheap. They prefer as few people working as possible."

"Oh well." Michael sighed.

After a moment, Sarah asked, "Something wrong?"

"Mom's in the hospital."

"Oh my God, what happened?"

"She has a bacterial infection. It's in her bloodstream, which is fairly serious. She's being treated in the ICU. It's supposedly under control. But then again, she's still in the ICU."

"Oh, Michael, I'm so sorry. Have you been to see her?"

"Yeah, went with my dad."

"How's he taking it?"

"Rough, as expected."

"I bet. You talk about the whole 'ignoring email' thing?"

"Yeah, was a little uneasy, but we smoothed things over."

"Oh good."

"You and Jack were right; I was a dick about it."

"Well at least you can admit it. How did it go, reconnecting?"

"Good, actually. Told him about the interview."

"Great. So things are good with you and them?"

"Getting better. It scared the shit out of me to see Mom like that: hooked up to tubes and wires... in that place."

"I'm so sorry."

"The ICU, Sarah. It's awful. Feels like everyone is on the brink of... something bad."

"Wow. Don't know what I'd do if my mom was in there. But you getting along with your parents is fantastic."

"I think getting a new job helped too."

"Wait. You got a new job?"

"Oh yeah--just today."

"Where?"

"Tech 4 U, I'm a technology consultant."

"Good for you! Hey, can you hook a sister up on a smart phone?"

"Hah! Always looking for the freebies. You radio people are all alike!"

"Yeah, well you're the guy always asking for concert tickets!"

They both laughed. Sarah said, "You need to come by the bar and catch a live band, or just hang out."

"Yes, gotta make that happen."

"We also need to catch up on *Stewardesses*, and well, I miss you!"

"Miss you too, Sarah. I'll come by soon."

"Alright! Well let me put my hellions to bed."

"Yep. Talk later!"

***

Michael arrived back at his apartment close to ten. He had

101

maybe another hour before Brad showed up back at the place to blare whatever action movie he was hot on that week.

He walked into several baskets of laundry around the house. Wash day, he mused. Brad must've ditched these to go to work. He scoured the kitchen, pulled out a loaf of bread, and made peanut butter sandwiches as he powered up his laptop.

The vision of his mom as she lay there connected to those tubes wasn't going to be easy to shake. It helped that he talked a little about it to Sarah. Maybe he needed more of that? He grabbed his phone.

"What's up?"

"Jack. Hey bro. Rough day."

"How?"

Michael took a bite of a sandwich. "Well for starters, mom's in the hospital."

"Oh no! Why?"

"Bacterial infection, bloodstream. She's in the ICU, man."

"Damn. How bad?"

"Bad. But they're treating her. Dad's been with her, and I'll go by when I can."

"Anything I can do?"

Michael pondered a minute. "No, but thanks. I'll let you know for sure."

"Heard about the Quicksolve job. I'm sorry."

"Yeah, me too. How'd you find out?"

"I asked."

"Well they called me."

"Oh okay."

"That was too quick, man. Did they know before I went in?"

"Dunno. They'd been interviewing for a few weeks."

"Should've let me know."

"Sorry again. I do have something to get your mind off that, however."

"Yeah, what's that?"

"Remember the airport jobs? Got one."

"Alright, buddy. Nice work."

"Thought you'd like that."

"A little money coming in? Sure. Oh and hey, I do have a little not so bad news too."

"What?"

"Got a job today."

"You holding out on me?"

"Maybe. It's Tech 4 U, store at Lakeside."

"Oh right, love that place."

"The owner came through my line the other day, and asked me to come by."

"Hey, nice step up, dude!"

"Sure thing. And I get to mess with gadgets. I'm happy."

"And maybe later, something at Quicksolve opens up."

"Not gonna hold my breath."

"Could happen."

"That's great. If it does, yeah, if not, I'm gonna keep looking. Besides, we have the limo world to conquer, right?"

"Yeah we do."

"So what's that limo pick up you mentioned?"

"Armstrong International, tomorrow 1pm."

***

"Watch where you're going!"

Michael's passenger yelled from the back seat as a car horn blared. The driver made sure they flipped Michael off as a courtesy.

"Sorry about that," Michael replied, half turned to the back. "Thought I had the light."

The man straightened his suit out. "Yeah well, I'd like to arrive at my hotel alive, if that isn't too much trouble." He frowned, and returned to his newspaper.

Canal street was busy with the remnants of the lunch rush still on the streets, not to mention crews had blocked off one lane of the street for construction. Do they ever stop working on streets in this town, Michael wondered.

He worked his way down to the Monteleone hotel, and was close. He promised he'd have returned to B&G in the next thirty minutes, so he still had time, as long as things sped up from this snail's pace they were at.

While he waited at a light, his mind wandered again back to the pilot seat of the 1960's clipper jet. *The plane wobbled through the air as random gusts shook the cabin. He checked the dials on the console, all looked well. Wait...maybe not. Fuel leak in one of the engines! The red warning light flashed, and before long he heard a whining sound coming from the starboard side of the plane.*

"Uh oh, trouble," his first officer remarked.

"Yeah, keep an eye on that. If the temperature runs too hot gonna have to shut it down."

Michael turned to the navigator. "How much further do we have?"

"Approximately 1300 miles, captain."

Michael looked at the co-pilot. "Can you tell how bad the fuel leak is?"

"I'm on it," the co-pilot remarked.

Just then the plane dipped wildly. Several screams rang from the back. He grabbed the intercom. "Ladies and gentlemen, this is your captain speaking. We'll be suspending drink service on this flight, and ask that you please remain seated for the duration. We apologize for the inconvenience."

A knock at the cabin door, and Leigh poked her head in. "You boys alright up here?"

"Not quite," Michael said. "Problem with an engine, may need to divert if it's bad enough."

Leigh nodded.

The whining sound came again. What was that?

"Not going to make our primary destination," the navigator replied. "Got an alternative, about 800 miles away. Should be fine with current fuel loss."

"What if we shut the engine down?" Michael offered.

"No, the leak can't be stopped. Looks like a bad fuel line, just happened to go mid air."

Quickly adjusting in his seat, Michael sighed in disgust. "Okay, so we're diverting." The whine again. But wait, it wasn't a whine, it sounded like something else.

"Do you guys hear that?" He asked the cockpit crew. They shook their heads.

The co-pilot quickly spun his head out the starboard window of the plane. Glancing back at Michael, he pointed and screamed, "Look out!!!"

At that moment, Michael realized what the sound was. It wasn't a whine, it was another car horn. The car lurched to the left as it was struck. The windows on the right side blew out. Michael grabbed the steering wheel tight, winced and hunched downward, as he anticipated another impact. The car came to a rest, though. A few seconds more and then Mr. Jones in the back seat groaned, and clasped his neck. Michael asked, "Are you alright?"

Even as he asked the question, he had an idea of the answer already. His face flushed and hot, he felt a surge of anxiety rush through him, and his skin prickled. It was as if everything around him was still going normal speed, but he was now in ultra low gear.

The man fumed, and grabbed his neck as if to staunch some pain. "You little bastard. You call this a limousine service? You're going to be hearing from my attorneys very soon."

"Sir, I'm sorry, it was an-"

"It was your fault, asshole," Jones yelled back. "You ran a red light, and they side swiped you."

Michael cringed. A low dull ache throbbed through his gut. This was awful. He had to call somebody. Jack. Had to get him in the know fast.

***

Michael sat on the corner of Canal and Decatur Street. The sun beat down on him, and it warmed the cool morning to a mildly pleasant temperature. If it wasn't for why he was standing here, it might have been a pleasant day. At least weather wise.

He broke the news to Jack. Jack didn't say much, but he was glad that Michael was okay. They were both nervous about Mr. Miller and the other driver. She was a college student, on her way to Tulane University. Michael gazed at the smashed front end of her Nissan. At least it wasn't a Porsche.

The town car wasn't drivable. The right side was smashed up, both windows blown out. After he spoke with police on the scene, Mr. Miller had himself checked by the paramedics, but not before he took the JM Limos info down, along with the insurance information. Michael dreaded possible thoughts of what that entailed. The girl waved off the paramedics. Mr. Miller asked to be taken to the hospital as he glanced sternly toward Michael.

As the ambulance drove away, Michael saw the girl was on her smart phone. She typed away as if in deep concentration. He slowly approached her. "I'm... sorry."

She jumped at his voice. She turned to him. "I really need to get to school."

"Sure you're okay?"

She nodded, though her taut lips and darting eyes suggested otherwise.

"Well I was going to get a cab. How about I get them to drop you off too?"

She glanced around. "Um, I don't think that's a good idea. But thanks."

"Sure?"

"I just have to call my friend." She nodded, smiled softly, then turned away, and walked toward the curb.

Michael called B&G. Mrs. Rose, annoyed by the news he'd be late, snipped at him. He figured he'd have lost an hour or two of pay by the time it was all over. And on top of the wreck. He sat on the curb, and called a cab while he hoped his head and life would just get settled for only a few moments.

Chapter Fourteen

Michael stood in front of a demonstration laptop at Tech 4 U, adjusted the screen resolution, and set up a demo video for customers. He was doing well there, more or less like Kenny had predicted. Sure was nicer than B&G.

It was strange, how he left his job at B&G after he had worked there for a few years. Even though there wasn't a future for him at the grocery, it had been an essential part of his life. It was a fairly amicable parting. Many of the cashiers at B&G only worked there for a few months during the summer or maybe a year or two. Michael was one of the longer term employees. Of course, the extra money from Tech 4 U and the tech gadgets made his departure easier.

It was a Tuesday afternoon, and the store was moderately crowded. Michael worked with a few other salespeople. After he set up the laptop, Michael returned to the main customer service desk where Kenny stood. "How's it going, Michael?" Kenny asked.

Michael placed a stack of smart phone brochures on the counter top. He looked at Kenny and replied, "Oh, just great, man. I'm so glad I took you up on this."

"Me too, you're a natural!"

"It's nice making money off talking about all this tech stuff I've been using for awhile anyway!"

Kenny laughed, "Yeah, loving what you do makes the job a helluva lot easier. Well, most of the time it does."

"Ya know, I almost got a job doing tech support not long ago. Glad I got this one."

"I had jobs doing tech support over the phone. I liked helping people, but there were always a few that were nasty as hell."

"Yeah, my buddy Jack was telling me some horror stories."

"I never could figure that out: I'm trying to help them with a problem that I had nothing to do with, and they're bitching me out."

Michael nodded.

Kenny continued, "One good thing about this business is there's not a lot of support we have to do. It's more about sales and recommending than troubleshooting and fixing."

Michael replied, "I gotcha. I'm getting better at the whole sales thing. At first I felt weird about pushing something on a complete stranger. Seemed like I'd be just telling them anything to get them to spend $900 on the latest tablet or something. But now I'm thinking it's more about just giving them advice."

Kenny said, "There you go. That's what I'm trying for here. I don't want people getting things shoved in their faces, and when they're home they realize they were screwed over. Not only will they not come back, but they'll tell everyone they know to stay away."

Michael smiled at Kenny. Kenny was obviously motivated to succeed at Tech 4 U, as the owner. Michael got a renewed desire to push forward in his life seeing how Kenny worked. He figured he may have found his way with this new job.

Now that Michael had employment, he thought about how his friends had more than jobs to sustain them. Even the short time he was there, Michael still sometimes had to duck out of Jack's apartment for him and Ashlyn's alone time. It served to remind him that he wasn't romantically involved with anyone.

A customer came up to the counter, and asked for recommendations on tablets. After he spoke with her for a few moments, the customer left. Michael turned to Kenny and said, "Going to see my mom in the hospital tonight."

"Uh oh, what happened?"

"Some kind of infection."

"Wow, sorry to hear that. How's she doing?"

"They moved her out of ICU about a week ago, but she's very groggy. Sleeps a lot. Not much energy."

"Well I hope that changes soon."

"Thanks!"

Michael checked the store for any customers who might have needed assistance. As he looked around, he noticed Jack walking up to the store entrance. Michael walked up to meet him at the entrance.

Jack extended his hand. "Well, if it isn't the smartphone pimp of Metairie?"

Michael reached his hand out, and shook Jack's. He replied, "Hey, don't get crazy and all calling me that just yet."

Jack smirked. "How's the town car?"

"Body shop says it will be a few more weeks."

"Hope it's soon, winter formals coming."

"It could be. They're looking for a door panel or something."

Jack nodded. "Nothing from insurance so far. I filed the claim, guess we'll see."

Michael sighed. "Sorry, man."

"Hey, just hope it doesn't get nasty with Mr. Miller."

"What if it does?"

Jack regarded him for a second, then diverted his gaze. Michael shook his head.

"So, how goes the gig, man? You're here what, three weeks?"

"More like two. Going fine."

"Better than slinging milk and veggies, huh?"

"Sure thing. Think I'm getting the hang of this sales thing."

"Not that bad, huh?"

"It's a lot easier when you're interested in what you're selling." Michael motioned, and walked toward a laptop display. "These babies are something else. Way faster than my own. Maybe one day I'll do my upgrade here."

Jack said, "Just don't blow your paycheck."

Michael nodded.

Jack said, "We should keep looking for limo clients."

"I'm gonna keep the word up on Facebook, hope we can get some more takers soon."

"Well, just wanted to say hi."

"Thanks for coming by."

"Sure, well let me go, dinner with Ashlyn."

"How are you getting along?"

"We're okay. Still trying to juggle her and my other ambitions. Only so much time."

"It'll work, man. At least that's what I keep telling myself."

"Not much on the motivation, huh?"

Michael shook his head. "It's tough when so much is falling apart around me. You know my dickhead roommate almost didn't pay our rent for the month?"

"What?"

"Yeah. I gave him my half like we agreed. Seems he figured it could wait til he maybe got lucky at Harrah's."

Jack winced. "He didn't... lose it gambling, huh?"

"Naah thank God. I got in touch with him, and he took care of the rent. If I hadn't, might be living on the sidewalk right now. Gotta get away from him as soon as possible."

"Kinda tough for you right now."

"And I just trashed our business car."

"Make it right!" Jack patted his shoulder.

"You sound like my boss."

"All right, back to work."

"Even more like my boss now. Hey, live music at Ales tomorrow, want to check it out? Sarah will be there."

"What time?"

"Probably ninish."

"Yeah, alright. I'll see if Ashlyn wants to go."

After their goodbyes, Michael busied himself with a customer who asked about laptops. In the back of his mind, he wondered what other risks he might take, like Jack and Kenny suggested. Oh well, he supposed he'd done enough for now, and another night of no action wouldn't hurt.

***

Michael heard a familiar voice behind him as he busied himself with a tablet display at Tech 4 U.

"Michael?"

He turned to see Chloe in her school uniform, with a smile on her face.

"Hey," he said. "Just off from school I see?"

She nodded, "Yeah. Look, Aunt Rose told me you left and were here now."

"Ah."

She shuffled a bit on her feet, biting her lip.

"What's up?"

"I, um, wanted to thank you, for what you did that night you drove us."

"Oh, the dance?"

She sighed, and ran her fingers through her long hair. "Yeah. Those guys were real jerks."

Michael nodded, and thought back a bit to his wild days, and the things he'd gotten into. Not like Chloe and Jamie's dates though. Even what they did hadn't really been worth it, from his experiences anyway. "Well I'm glad I could help. Y'all don't need that around you."

She smiled at him. "No. Guess I'll see you around?"

Michael studied her. "Maybe. If you need a new smartphone sometime, look me up."

"Oh I will," she chuckled. They hugged, and she left. Michael smiled to himself. *Guess I can still get a few things right now and then,* he thought.

***

Band night at Ales quickly became very popular in the several months of its existence. Sarah and the rest of the bar staff were very happy with the extra money, although the hustle it required left them drained by the end of the night. Sarah hoped she could take it easy the next morning. As long as her boys weren't out to start World War III. She had left them with her mom and

111

expectations of their better behavior for grandma.

The band started at ten. Michael, Jack and Ashlyn arrived shortly after nine. Jack grabbed a seat at the almost packed bar for Ashlyn, while he and Michael stood behind her.

Ashlyn looked around and said, "Wow, nice crowd!"

Jack commented, "Amazing what a little live music does for business.

"Which band?" Ashlyn asked.

"Tourniquet," Michael chimed in. "According to the flyer, they're a hard rock group."

"Tourniquet?" Ashlyn asked, with a slight wince. "Hard rock?"

"Humm, 'hard'--I bet you use that word a lot, Ashlyn," quipped Michael.

Looking at him with mild disgust, she retorted, "Maybe if you went on a date every now and then, you might actually hear it too."

Jack and Michael guffawed at Ashlyn's comeback. Michael placed his hand on her shoulder and said, "I knew there was a reason I liked you. Well done!"

As Ashlyn rolled her eyes, Jack shook his head, and averted his gaze to behind the bar. Sarah handled drink orders as they flew across the bar like mosquitoes at cars on a highway. She glanced briefly at Jack, and waved.

Jack stroked Ashlyn's shoulders. Michael looked around the bar, and then glanced toward the stage area. Jack commented, "It's 9:30 and the band's just setting up."

Michael replied, "More time to drink while we wait."

Ashlyn and Jack looked toward the stage as well. Jack replied, "Well I heard a few weeks back one group didn't get on til quarter to eleven."

They were slightly startled when Sarah blurted out behind them, "Why the hell are y'all looking over there? The real show's back here!"

Jack and Michael faced Sarah, still behind the bar and with her hands on her hips. Ashlyn waved to Sarah, which Sarah acknowledged when she nodded quickly and blinked.

Michael said, "Hey girl, good to see you. What's the microbrew of the month?"

"It's got some long convoluted name. If you were more of a bar snob, I'd get my cheat sheet and rattle it off to you, but how about I pour you some?"

Michael replied, "Sounds good to me."

Sarah turned to Jack and Ashlyn. "What about you guys?"

Jack leaned forward and said, "I'll have a Guinness, and Ashlyn here will have a Cosmopolitan." He turned to Ashlyn and said, "That's right, huh?" She nodded in agreement.

Sarah went to get their drinks. Ashlyn looked at Michael and said, "So, Michael, how's the new job?"

"Not bad. Two weeks, and they haven't fired me yet. No, seriously, it's a neat place."

"What's the place?"

"Tech 4 U."

"Oh right, saw them in the mall."

"Dunno if this one will be a long-term job, but at least I'm dealing with something I already know and care about. So how's the accounting life, Ashlyn?" Michael asked.

"Not bad. It has its moments, but it's a career, and my boss seems to like me."

"You like it?"

"It's alright. I won't lie and say I'm head over heels in love with it, though." She smirked.

"Must be nice, having a regular schedule and weekends off," Michael marveled.

"It suits me okay, enough so I'm not bored all day, but not so in love that I bring work home to do at night or over the weekend."

"Well sure."

"I like making a living and having time for fun, you know?"

Michael said, "My dad has been on me to find something I love to do, so I can build a career."

"Well that helps, but not everyone gets there," Ashlyn said.

"I just don't know if there's any kind of work that I could totally and completely love."

Ashlyn replied, "I don't think that's a bad thing. You've got to find a balance, at least I feel you do. If you spend all your time working or all your time just having fun, you're missing out on something."

Sarah returned with their drinks. Michael raised his to clink against Ashlyn's glass. "Thanks, Ashlyn. And I was only kidding about the 'hard' thing."

Ashlyn smirked. "If I'm not used to it by now I'll never be. Besides, I don't have virgin ears."

Tourniquet took the stage. They were a hard rock band, all right. The people who sat at the tables toward the front of the stage immediately leaned back from the amps. Jack, Michael, and Ashlyn were a good fifteen feet away from them, but they still felt the sound as it thumped them in their chests.

Jack yelled into Michael's ear, "Little more of this, and I might need a tourniquet or something.

"Yeah?"

"My chest gave in a little on their first chord."

Michael replied, "You nut." They laughed and clinked glasses.

The band played for a solid two hours before taking a break. Michael watched Sarah, her petite frame as she glided back and forth behind the bar with subtle grace. She busily filled drink orders. If there were a reality TV show called *Do You Think You Can Be a Dancing Bartender*, Sarah would be an excellent contestant, Michael mused to himself.

Michael smiled as he watched Sarah's torso as she leaned over to take drink orders, and then quickly spun around to grab a fresh, cold glass and proceeded to a beer tap. Moments later she headed to the nearest cooler, retrieved a bottle, and whipped out her opener from her back pocket. For some brief moments, Michael wondered if he and Sarah could be more than friends. Jack noticed something, for sure. Michael quickly stopped his mind from thoughts of that as he said to himself, *We're just friends, and I'm certainly not ready to be a father.*

On her break, Sarah stood nearby the group. Michael held up his hand and said, "You're working it like a champ! High-five!"

Sarah slapped his hand, and managed a quick mock curtsy. "Thanks, babe. So what about the band?"

Ashlyn glanced around at Jack and said, "They're loud", and then added, "Guess it's not our taste in music, but the company's great." Michael nodded in agreement.

Sarah shrugged. "Yeah, the bands we get are hit or miss. Overall, band night has been a huge boost to this girl's take-home pay. And that, more than anything, makes for a happy Sarah." She danced a bit, her face giddy.

Michael shook his head at her antics. "Okay, we get it. You only love us for our money."

Sarah replied, "Hold it. It's not just for your money. It's for a lot of your money!"

"Gah, all this time, and that's all I'm good for?"

"Well, you also have great taste in TV shows about 1960s air travel."

Ashlyn sighed, "Again with the *Stewardesses*!" She looked at Jack with a smile. Jack nodded, and stroked her arm gently he replied, "Oh come on. You can join in on our chats, Facebook and otherwise!" Ashlyn rolled her eyes, and patted Jack on the cheek.

Sarah nudged Michael, and chimed in, "And you could always log in to Twitter and have 'ol Michael here flirt with you as Captain Tim the pilot!"

Ashlyn and Michael turned to look at Sarah, who giggled. Ashlyn said, "Oh, I'm on Twitter already! Wait, Michael, are you into that role play stuff on there?"

"Yeah, you could say that."

"Nice, I don't do that, but some of my girlfriends do. They have accounts on other show characters."

"Lots of people into that."

"I'll have to check yours out. What's the username?"

"@Tim707."

Jack said, "I need to get on Twitter once and for all. You do that, Sarah?"

"Hah!" Sarah scoffed. "Facebook is where it's at for me. I like posting pics of my babies, and Facebook just makes it easier."

"It's not the whole deal though," Michael retorted. "Twitter rocks!"

Sarah held a hand to Michael. "I can swoon over the hot guys on *Stewardesses* while fanboy Michael here Tweets his ass off. Twitter seems a little too much trouble to me."

Michael sneered. "Oh, you'd love Twitter if you gave it a shot!"

Sarah smiled, "Maybe."

Ashlyn kissed Jack on the cheek. Sarah glanced back toward

the stage. "They're about to start the second set. Catch up with y'all when it's over."

The second set wasn't as long as the first, though Michael, Jack and Ashlyn were in agreement that it was long enough. Once the show was over, the three of them ordered one more round before the bar had last call. The crowd steadily thinned out after the band left the stage. Sarah's frenetic pace slowed down soon afterward, and she wiped down the counter, close to Michael and the others.

Michael said, "You know, we should hang out together someplace other than this bar."

"Wait, there's other places besides here?" Jack winked.

"I mean it. We should hang out when Sarah isn't working, so she can hang out too. What do you think, Sarah?"

Sara folded the bar cloth as she listened to Michael. "That sounds fine; Just need to figure out my schedule."

Sarah's "yes" gave Michael a buzz.

Ashlyn added, "That could be fun. Maybe a day at the lakefront would be nice."

Jack nodded. "Talk about it later, I'm exhausted."

Just at that moment, Sarah's cell phone rang. She pulled it out to see her mom's number on the caller id. "Hang on, I have an idea, but I need to make sure my sons haven't committed murder and mayhem at Grandma's house."

Jack and Ashlyn sat down at bar stools as they waited for Sarah to finish her call. Michael stretched a bit. They watched Sarah's expression as it changed from mild curiosity to one of grave concern on the phone as she slowly ran through several questions, "Are you sure, Mom? How long ago did it happen? Do they know what caused it?"

Sarah hung up the phone, and abruptly tossed it on the bar. "Well that's just fucking great. How do you like that?"

"What happened?" Asked Jack.

Sarah took a deep breath, and closed her eyes for a moment. She opened them, and looked at Michael. "Apparently, Kelly had a seizure while in school in New York. It happened while she was in class. They have her at a hospital up there."

"Oh my God," replied Michael. "Is she alright?"

"I don't know. Mom gave me the info she has, which isn't a

whole lot. I don't know what she has in the way of insurance, but... this is just... not fair." Sarah slapped her hand on the bar, her eyes downward. Suddenly the words her mom said rang true. Kelly indeed had her own circumstances to deal with. And Kelly was up there, alone.

"What are you gonna do?" Asked Michael.

Sarah glanced sharply at Michael. "Well I just found out, so I don't really know yet. I know we've got to do something."

Michael watched as Sarah wrung her hands and glanced around the bar. It was like she tried for any distraction she could, so whatever meltdown of hers wouldn't happen.

"I gotta figure this out. She's my big sister. I can't just let her handle this alone. She needs me."

Michael placed his hand on the bar near Sarah. "Well, let me know if I can help. Okay?"

"That goes for me too," added Jack. Ashlyn nodded in support.

"Thanks, guys. Let me get together with mom, and see how we're going to handle this. I will keep y'all up to date on what's happening."

They finished their drinks, and left the bar.

***

As Michael drove home, his thoughts wandered to Sarah. How much could one person - should one person - have handled alone? When he got back to his apartment, he called Jack. "That's something about Sarah's sister, isn't it?"

"Yeah,"

"Always seemed like a nice girl."

"Don't remember her having seizures."

Michael thought a moment. "She's going up there if she has to walk the whole way."

"Can she, with her kids and two jobs?"

"She's gonna find a way."

"Tough spot for her."

"She's not in a great place for a trip, but that's not the issue. Her sister needs her. Remember that *Stewardesses* when Monique began searching for her long lost brother? She cared so much

117

about learning about her past, and reconnecting with her sibling. It was very important to her. Sarah cares about the people in her life. She'll do the same thing, reaching out for her family however she can."

Jack asked Michael, "So you still deny there's anything between you two?"

"Come on, not now."

"Dude. I saw you looking at her tonight."

"Yeah, and?"

"You couldn't keep your eyes off her. Even Ashlyn saw you checking her out."

"What? I can't look at my friend working behind the bar?"

"I don't look at any of my friends like that."

"The girl's a little sister to me, man!"

"Hey, she's attractive, and you know she's cool. If I was single, I'd give it a shot."

"Oh that's nice, Jack. I'm sure Ashlyn would love to hear that."

"You know what I mean. Wouldn't blame you if you started something with her."

"Well, now that I have your permission... that changes everything."

Jack scoffed "I tried."

Satisfied that Jack had dropped the subject, Michael pulled out his laptop. He logged onto Facebook, and checked the *Stewardesses* page for more updates. He noticed that some fans of Charlotte had visited a location shoot for *Stewardesses*, and they posted a picture of them with the actress. Michael opened the picture file to see Charlotte, dressed in her outfit from the show. She showed her classic million dollar smile, her arms around two people in their street clothes who also grinned wildly.

Given the growing internet buzz about *Stewardesses* not being renewed for a second season, it felt even more like his chances to see a live shoot were very limited. He'd have to act quick.

"Hey," Michael said. "Charlotte's been out taking pics with fans of the show in New York."

"Having all the fun while they can."

"We should make a trip to New York."

"What, now?"

"Yeah, I mean it'd be perfect. Help Sarah and Kelly, and maybe meet some... other people."

"Isn't that beyond your means? We haven't gotten past the wreck yet."

"I know. But think about it. It makes sense to me. Sarah would just about sell her kidney to get up there. Why not help Sarah get to New York to help her sister?"

"And you happen to stalk Charlotte Ducrest on a shoot for *Stewardesses*?"

"I'd be up there already and everything," Michael grinned.

"Am I in a romantic comedy right now?" Jack mused.

"Gimme a break. When my mom got sick, you think my dad hesitated for one second? Sarah's sister doesn't have anyone up there. Sure, it'd be great to meet Charlotte, but I'm thinking of Sarah here. She never asks anyone for anything. She has a lot on her shoulders, and she needs a helping hand for a change."

While Michael often didn't have a clear direction on choices he made in life, this idea of Sarah quickly became fixed in his mind as a mission, a direction for him. It felt good, better than what had come his way so far. To Michael, it seemed perfect: Kelly and Sarah were helped, and just maybe he'd have gotten his life figured out in the process.

Jack was a little less idealistic. "Michael, she's got her mom to help."

"Yeah?"

"It's real nice of you, but don't you think her family would figure out a way to take care of this?"

"Sarah works two jobs, as you've noticed. Her mom works a part time job but isn't exactly rolling in cash either."

"I know."

"They need extra help."

"What makes it have to be you?"

"Feels like something I need to do."

"I dunno."

"It's not just a trip. It's helping Sarah."

"What about the limo business?"

"It won't be for long. I'm worried about her, alright? Her boys, her sister and her mom are all she has. She needs support now."

Jack countered, "Think about yourself. Your new job. I don't think your boss would care for you skipping work for a week, maybe more?"

"Maybe not."

"Definitely not. They wouldn't play this at Quicksolve. Not your first weeks on the job, anyway."

"Good thing I'm not at Quicksolve then."

"What if Quicksolve comes back with something?"

"Look, I'm helping this girl."

"What about your mom?"

Michael paused. "She's in a regular room. They say she's getting better."

"Maybe. But what if after you're gone she gets worse?"

"I need to try. Mom has dad. Sarah needs help."

Jack sighed. "And the fact this actress you're lusting after is in the same vicinity has no bearing on this decision?"

Michael scratched his head for a moment. "Maybe... look, what would you do? Don't you feel sorry for her?"

"Of course. Single mom, piece of shit baby daddy, and a sister out of state who needs her help."

"I need to do this."

"Are you worried about the accident?"

"Sure."

"Maybe at least think it out more first?"

"No time."

"Is this really about your friend?"

Michael scratched his head for a moment. "It is."

"Mmmhmm, and you won't try and see Charlotte since you'll happen to be nearby?"

"That's not why I'm going. It'll be a quick shot, hopefully, maybe a week, and then I'll return, and be right where I started."

"Or behind."

"I'm helping a friend though, that is the bigger thing here."

"Just make sure it's about Sarah and Kelly first. My two cents."

"Okay, got you. Guess I'm wondering if this will open my mind up."

"What do you mean?"

"Change my perspective, new city, away from what I'm doing."

"Not sure."

"Even if it doesn't, I'm helping a really good friend, and I think I can live with that."

"It's an awful expensive risk, man."

"Several hundred in gas, plus a hotel room here and there. I figure with stops for gas, food, and to sleep, it'll take us around three days one way, maybe a little less if we drive through the night, and only get a room every other day or so. I'll figure something out."

They ended the call. Michael stayed up a while longer. He glanced at the photo of Charlotte for a moment. *Okay, it would be nice to meet her,* he thought. Then he pulled up Sarah's Facebook profile, and put her pic side by side with Charlotte. Two women, one an imagined ideal, the other someone who pervaded his mind more each day.

Chapter Fifteen

Michael went to Ales the next evening. The bar was far less crowded than when the band was there. Sarah watched one of the big screen TVs while she tended to the four people at the bar. When she caught sight of Michael she smiled, and waved him over to an empty stool.

Michael leaned forward and said, "Hey, good looking!"

Sarah grinned and replied, "Hey you."

They hugged, and Michael gave her a peck on the cheek. He sat down on the barstool, and ordered a beer. When Sarah returned, he asked, "How's Kelly?"

"Still in the hospital. Had another seizure, and they don't want to release her just yet."

"Shit."

"Yeah. She's excused from classes, rest of this semester and next."

"Wow, the whole year?"

"Unless she gets cleared before."

"Least she doesn't have to worry about school, right?"

"Yeah, but her financial aid won't stay in effect while she isn't attending classes, so she needs to move out of student housing."

"Ugh."

"I wish I could do something for her."

Michael sipped his beer, set it on the bar, and looked at Sarah for a moment. "I have an idea."

"Oh?"

"What if you made a trip to see her, and helped her while her medical condition gets resolved?"

Sarah gazed at Michael. "I'd love to. Been trying to figure out how."

"I'm not saying it would be easy. But I can help you."

"That's really sweet, Michael, but didn't you just start a new job?"

Michael chuckled. "I want to help you, Sarah. It happens there's a TV show I wanted to check out in New York, around this time."

Sarah arched her eyebrow, folding her arms. "Okay... what are you talking about now?"

"See, *Stewardesses* is still doing location shoots in New York..."

Sarah raised her hand up, and laughed. "*Stewardesses*? Why am I not surprised? Always with the gawking." She shook her head.

"No, no."

Sarah smirked. Michael added, "Fine, I like Charlotte. But Kelly needs your help. And I know you're strapped a bit. Let me help here."

Sarah shook her head. "And in the process you happen to ogle this woman?"

"Maybe I do, maybe I don't. Won't have much more of a chance now that they're canceling the series."

Sarah's eyes widened in mock fright. "Now what are you gonna do?"

"It's a show. Yeah, sucks it may get canceled."

"I thought you said the Save *Stewardesses* thing was working. I did a few of those petitions like you mentioned."

"Well, seems it isn't working enough."

Sarah sauntered off to get someone's drink, then returned to stand in front of Michael. "You know, my hoopty car will probably not make it up there."

"It's okay. Mine's newer and as long as you can chip in some for gas we should be fine."

She looked past him for a moment, her brow furrowed in thought. "Okay, Michael. You're on."

"Alright!"

"But one condition: we help Kelly first. Once we have her set up somewhere, you can go on your little Charlotte Easter Egg Hunt. But not before, got it?"

"Agreed."

"I mean it."

"Don't worry, I'm not as into her as you think I am."

They both laughed. Sarah said, "Yeah, right."

"Uh huh, whatever." He shook his head, grinning.

Sarah studied Michael. "You'd do that, huh? For me?"

"Figured y'all need the help, especially if she has to move."

"If I can just be there for her in person, that's huge. Whatever we need to do up there." Her voice wavered as she added, "Gotta be quick... so I can get back." She cocked her head a moment, sniffled and hoped Michael hadn't noticed the tear before her hand wiped it.

"Absolutely. No problem."

"Thank you so much, Michael. This... means so much."

Michael drank more of his beer while Sarah tended to the other people at the bar. Every time he'd gone over the trip idea, it seemed right. Sarah and Jack may have had their suspicions, but Michael just knew this was the right move for him.

As he drank his beer, Michael felt a sharp slap on his right shoulder. He turned and saw Jack. Jack simply said, "Partner?"

Turning to embrace Jack, Michael said, "How are you, buddy?"

"Good. Glad you're around."

"Sit down."

Jack sat on a barstool, and ordered a Guinness from Sarah. "Been thinking about your trip idea."

"Yeah?"

"I've looked into some crazy businesses. A lot ended up as one dead end scam or another."

"Okay?" Michael shifted in his seat.

"And I think sometimes just looking for the right idea helps me out."

Michael smiled and nodded.

Jack continued, "I want you to move to the next level. But the way you talk about helping Sarah, you've got this fire in you. Like you're determined."

Michael tipped his glass. "Well yeah, now that you mention it."

"What I'm trying to say is that I respect that."

"Thanks."

"I know you kinda have some other ideas about why you're going up there." Jack arched an eyebrow. "Like you said, this is about helping Sarah and Kelly. They mean a lot to me too, so I'm gonna help y'all."

Stunned by this sudden turn of generosity, Michael stammered and finally said, "Man, that's...that's great. Thanks, Jack."

Michael hugged Jack as they sat on their stools. Michael said, "You know I'm going to pay you back, right?"

Jack nodded and said, "I know."

Sarah returned with Jack's beer. "What did I miss?"

Michael replied, "I have the two best friends in the world."

Sarah smiled and said, "Funny I was thinking the same thing."

"Jack's gonna chip in for us getting to New York."

Sarah's eyes flickered as her voice shook. "Jack, that's so sweet."

Jack patted her hand. "Of course."

Sarah sighed, and composed herself. "Thank you both for this."

"Well," Michael slammed his hand on the bar. "What are we waiting for?"

Sarah said, "Gotta figure out my work schedule and kids while we're away."

Michael replied, "And there's my employer. Maybe he'll give me a few days off."

"Michael, you really sure about this?" Sarah asked

"I am."

"Y'all may end up eating Thanksgiving dinner on the road," Jack commented.

"I - we're going," Michael said.

"Might be tough," Jack replied. "What if your boss says no?"

"I guess I'll take what happens. Don't want to lose my job, but on the other hand, if I don't see this through, think I'll feel the worse for it."

Sarah glanced at Michael. "Wait, you might get fired if you take off for this? Michael, no. I'll figure out a way if I need to alone."

"Hey, enough alright? I'm doing this. I thought it through." Michael glanced at Jack. Jack shrugged, and winked at Sarah as she smiled.

Sarah looked at Jack and back to Michael. "Well okay, maybe they'll give you some slack. Play up the sick person visit thing, maybe that will ease it a little."

Michael finished his beer, and motioned to Sarah to pour him another. Jack said, "Hope it works out."

Michael shrugged. He was glad for Jack's support. "Thanks, Jack."

Jack took a sip of his beer and asked, "Told your dad yet?"

Michael replied, "No. Maybe in another day or so."

***

As Michael drove to his parents' house the next day, he planned his approach of Kenny about time off from Tech 4 U. He wasn't scheduled to work until 5pm that afternoon, so he had a few hours to plan things out. He was hopeful that Kenny would honor his request, though deep down he feared he may have to sacrifice his job. In spite of that, he held on to the belief that this trip was something he needed to do.

He expected a strong reaction from them against this trip. If Jack and even Sarah raised objections, he figured his parents would be even more vocal. In any case, he lived on his own now. Their opinion wasn't going to deter him.

Michael entered the house to find his dad at the kitchen table, with coffee. John greeted Michael, his arms held out to embrace him. "Hey, my boy! How are you doing?"

"Good." Michael replied cheerfully. "How's mom?"

As they sat down John replied, "Hanging tough. She was awake for a little while last night, but they're keeping her sedated. Her fever hasn't broken yet."

Michael nodded.

"Want some coffee?" John asked.

"Sure."

As John poured, Michael asked, "So do they have any idea how long she'll be there?"

"Not sure, son. They've been switching out antibiotics, and keep thinking they've found one but no."

John placed Michael's coffee cup on the table. He went back to grab the milk, sugar and artificial sweetener. Michael watched his father prepare the table with coffee accoutrements and said, "You're making me feel like I should be tipping you."

John laughed. "Well you know I like recognition. So, how're things going? How's the new job?"

"It's better than B&G, that's for sure."

"You and that laptop of yours were always inseparable around here."

"Sure thing." Michael took a sip and added, "Actually, there's something you should know about."

John perked up. "What's that?"

Michael paused for a moment. "Remember my friend, Sarah?"

"Not sure."

"She has the two kids, works at that bar?"

"Oh wait the one with the green hair and tattoos?"

"Blue, actually."

"What about her?"

"Well she's got a sister, Kelly, in New York. The other day, she had a seizure and is up in the hospital there."

"Aww that's bad, how does this involve you?"

"I'm gonna go help Sarah take care of her."

"Take care of her?"

"Well, visit her in the hospital, make sure she's alright."

"What about your job here?"

"Not sure, hoping I can get a few days off."

"Can't her family help out?"

"She doesn't have anyone else up there, and her only family is

127

Sarah and their mom. They are strapped for cash to make a trip there to help Kelly, so I'm going to help them out."

John shook his head slightly. "Son, you really think that's a good idea... at this point? You're trying to establish yourself on your own. A trip like this could set you back. I know you want to help your friend, but sometimes you need to help yourself first. You know, you're just starting to be self sufficient."

Michael said, "I know, dad. But please hear me out."

John set his coffee cup on the table, and folded his arms. "You just started another job. What if you lose it over this? It's not very responsible, son. Sarah's family can find a way."

"They can't. Dad, I need to do this."

"And what about your mom? She's doing okay now, but I don't know if that's going to change. Suppose she gets worse while you're away and..." His voice trailed off as he shook his head and pushed any dreadful thoughts out.

"I know you don't think it's a good idea. And yeah, mom being like this right now scares me."

"What if I need you for something? Ever think of that?"

"Dad, this isn't easy. I'm sorry I'll be out, but it's just a week, maybe a little more."

John scoffed, then stirred his coffee as Michael continued. "Look I've been feeling, for a while, that there's something else for me: something I should be doing, and I can't figure out what it is."

John replied, "Don't you realize I... we... are just concerned for you? I'm sure your mother would back me up here."

Michael leaned back in his chair. "I know. I'm sorry."

John eyed Michael a moment. "You know, one of the things I learned in the AA meetings was about facing responsibilities. It's great, helping friends. But you have a job and bills of your own, son."

"But think about how you reached out to help mom when she got sick. I want to do that for my friend. She needs me. I know you're concerned for me, and I appreciate and love you for that, but if I can't try, fail, and try again, be my own man, what good am I?"

Michael took another drink of coffee. John said, "I'm sorry too, Michael. I guess I still think of you as our little boy who I'm trying to protect from the world. I don't agree with this plan of yours, but you're your own man."

Michael nodded. John continued, "I'll make you a deal: I'll try to give you more space if you'll at least hear me out when I have advice for you."

Michael pondered his offer, then replied, "That sounds fine."

John said, "Okay, now what about your job?"

"Well, I'm not sure. I'm asking him for several days off and hoping for the best."

John nodded. "Might go pretty bad."

Michael said, "I know. But as strong as I feel about doing this, about making this trip, I also know it might cost me my job. And I've borrowed money from Jack and will be behind on paying that debt to him."

"Well, I still think it's a big risk, son. I hope you don't expect me to help you out if you get into money trouble here."

"I know."

"I can see you're determined, and I must say I admire your conviction."

Michael replied, "I think I got that from my dad."

They laughed. After they finished their coffee, they ordered take-out for dinner, and ate at the house. Michael felt relieved he was on better terms with his dad. More than that, Michael was proud of himself he held his ground, regardless of anyone else's evaluation of his plan. He only hoped his mom would be able to tell him herself one day.

***

Michael waited his entire shift before he spoke with Kenny. The store was especially busy that day, and Michael tried to avoid Kenny all morning and early afternoon. He figured it would be better he waited until the end of the day. He had no idea what Kenny's reaction would be. Kenny took an interest in Michael and seemed, for the most part, very supportive since Michael started this job.

As his shift ended, Michael approached Kenny and asked, "Can I talk to you a sec?"

Kenny carried laptop computer in a box. He nodded to the

door in the back and replied, "In my office." He set the laptop box down by a display, and they walked to the back of the store.

Kenny's office was small and not really meant to be occupied for very long. A square-shaped room, there was just enough space for a desk, two chairs and a shelving unit that held some binders with training materials and employee paperwork.

Kenny sat at the chair behind his desk, and Michael sat down in the other chair, which was near the door. Michael slowly shut the door. Kenny took out his smart phone and muted the sound. He glanced at Michael. "Alright?"

Michael tensed up. This was the moment he'd waited for and dreaded. The unknown was before him. Even though he was committed to this trip, the uncertainty of his future at his job was painful for him.

Michael spoke slowly, "I know I haven't been here long, but I need to take a few days off."

Kenny frowned a bit. He asked, "What's wrong? Something happen to your mom?"

"No, I need time off to visit someone out of state. They're in New York, so it's gonna take at least a week, maybe a little more."

Kenny leaned back in his chair and studied Michael. His frown remained. He glanced downward a moment, then back at Michael, and said, "Ten years ago, I was a waiter in a Mexican restaurant. It was a moderately good place. The pay wasn't great--all right, it sucked. I stayed with the job because I thought maybe if I impressed the owner, he might make me manager one day."

Michael leaned back in his chair, and nodded in thought.

Kenny continued, "Well, one night the owner calls me into his office. Here it is, I think I've got my big break, and the manager's position is all mine. He didn't give it to me. He tells me his son-- who is lazy and a jackass and hasn't done half of the work I'd done around the restaurant--is going to be the new manager. That was it for me. I quit that night. In hindsight, quitting wasn't the smartest thing to do. I had recently gotten married, and we were living paycheck to paycheck. But quitting was better for me in the long run, because it gave me the kick in the ass to change myself. I was forced to start off on my own, to see what I could do by myself."

Michael managed just a "Wow" in response.

Kenny regarded him sternly for a moment. "Point I'm getting at is, yeah, sometimes ya gotta make tough choices in life. But I was thinking about my future. This friend of yours, I'm sure they're great people. But you're ditching a job to help them out - I dunno. I saw something in you, Michael. That's why you're here now."

"I know, and I appreciate that," Michael answered. "I thought this through, and my friends don't really have anyone else right now."

Kenny sighed. "I get it. But you gotta see it from my side too. I don't have twenty people I can just call to get a fill in for you until you're back."

"I know," Michael replied, his eyes falling.

He said, "I offered you this job because you seemed like a bright kid going nowhere."

"Yeah, and I'm grateful, but-"

Kenny interrupted, "I'm giving you the chance to develop your ability here, Michael. But there's one other ability you need to work on, and that's depend-ability."

Michael replied, "I know. I just really need to do this."

Kenny's hands shot up. "Well, Michael, I said my piece. That's it; I can't let you go."

Michael felt a sharp pain. He'd sacrificed his job if he took this trip. *Was it really worth it*, he wondered. *I've got to try*. His mind flashed to an episode of *Stewurdesses*, where Leigh, the lead stewardess was working as a waitress at a diner and decided to walk out on that job for a chance at a better opportunity: becoming a stewardess and traveling the world. While she had no offers and no real plan for a job at the airline, she figured that if she didn't take that risk she would have languished in the diner, and her life would not have gone anywhere. Michael figured that in spite of all the unknowns, this had to be worth it in the end.

Michael said, "I'm sorry, Kenny."

Kenny shook his head and stared at Michael. Then, he quickly stood up from his chair, turned around to face the shelf on the wall behind his desk and rifled through a file. He retrieved a sealed window envelope. He turned back around to Michael, and said, "Here's your check. I'll send the last one to your mailing address.

Leave your name tag before you go."

Michael took the check and slowly removed his name tag. He placed the name tag on Kenny's desk, and looked at it briefly. He looked back up at Kenny, who had averted his eyes. Kenny muttered, "I hope you find what you're looking for, Michael. Just remember, sometimes to find your way you need to finish what you start." Kenny glanced at Michael and nodded toward his office door.

Michael rose from his chair, exited Kenny's office and left Tech 4 U. With his paycheck and the money he borrowed from Jack, he had enough to travel and to stay a few days at a modest hotel.

Well, it was done now. He was free.

Michael arrived at his apartment at a quarter to eleven that evening. He called Jack.

"What's up?"

"You can say 'I told you so' now."

"Huh?"

"Asked my boss for time off and lost my job."

"Sorry. Had to be done, right?"

"Yeah, I guess. Well, I have the bucks for the trip, so that's it. Nothing left to hold me back."

"Something's gonna turn up."

"Yeah, if I can wait that long."

"Maybe another opening at Quicksolve. And when town car is back we're hitting the streets again."

"Don't want to think about that right now."

"How's your cash situation?"

"Well, thanks to your loan, what I have in savings, and hopefully a little from Sarah, we should be able to swing meals and a few nights of hotel stays, provided we avoid the Ritz Carlton type places."

"You never struck me as a four star kinda guy anyway."

"Cute. Well I'm going to pay you back. Before he let me go, Kenny talked about being dependable. I'm not going to let you down."

Jack grinned. "Good!"

Michael pulled out his laptop to figure out directions to New York. He asked Jack, "So how are things on your end?"

Jack shrugged, "Ashlyn's working longer hours. Quicksolve is going through some growing pains; just got some more sites to support, so more headaches and customers eager to vent. Oh well, it's job security, right?"

Michael replied, "Never say 'job security' to the guy who just got fired."

Jack laughed. "Right. Don't worry, your plan's in place. What's next?"

"Well, after a good night's sleep, we head out tomorrow morning. I'm figuring three to four days travel time to New York, so probably a few hotel stays or maybe we can kind of squat at a truck stop here and there."

"Alright."

"Once we get to New York, figure out Kelly's situation, and get that taken care of. And then... extracurricular activities."

"You know, in spite of my misgivings, gotta say I'm jealous you may meet Charlotte Ducrest."

Michael smiled. "I just hope Sarah can make arrangements for Kelly while we're there. Hey, keep an eye on Facebook, I'll keep you posted when we get there, and let you know how it goes."

Jack said, "Great. Good luck, my friend! The friendly skies await!"

Chapter Sixteen

Sarah sat at her desk at WZEB. The morning proposal drafts and account requests were piled up on her desk.

Just another frantic Monday.

She glanced at the stack of paperwork for a moment, and imagined it glared back at her and taunted her. She glanced at her computer screen, and looked at an email sent from Peter to the sales staff.

November 9
From: Peter Bloonan
To: WZEB Sales
RE: Live Broadcast Catering and Giveaways

Effective immediately, requests for food and prizes for food at live broadcasts MUST be submitted at minimum three days in advance, or your live broadcast will be canceled. We must get better about station events, so we don't look like idiots in front of our customers.

Sarah smirked. She wondered who had screwed up this time,

to prompt such a rebuke. Moments like this made her thankful she at least didn't have a radio salesperson's hassle to add to her workload.

Since the email had just been received, she figured she had a few minutes before Peter left for the morning for sales calls of his own. She leaned out the entrance to her cubicle and saw into Peter's office, where he glanced at his screen, seemingly engrossed.

She strode out of her cubicle, and walked quickly to Peter's office. Peter usually had something going on, whether it was email or a phone call, so Sarah figured she had to jump on him when the chance presented itself.

Sarah knocked on Peter's open office door. "Got a second?"

Peter glanced up. "Sure, what's up?" He leaned back in his chair, folding his hands across his chest.

Sarah walked to a nearby chair in front of Peter's desk and sat down. "I think I told you about my sister, the one in New York?"

"I think so. Isn't she an artist or something?"

"Culinary school, actually. She had a seizure and is in the hospital up there."

"Oh no, that's terrible!"

"Yeah, well my family is kind of scrambling to help her. We don't have any relatives up there, and it's just me and my mom to check on her."

"I see."

"I'm just not going to be okay until I know she's alright."

Peter nodded. Sarah continued, "I need to make a trip up there to help her sort everything out."

Peter pondered Sarah's words for a moment. He then leaned forward, his face showing concern. "Yeah, you need to take care of this. You have any vacation time saved up?"

"A few days, maybe a week, I think."

"No problem. I'll get someone to cover for you while you're out."

Sarah was surprised. She figured Peter would've approved her time off to help Kelly, but only after he added some catch for himself somewhere in the request. That wasn't the case in this instance. "Wow, thanks a lot, Peter!"

"Sure thing. When are you leaving town?"

"I don't know, maybe in a few days."

"Okay, well I'll work on getting an intern or something to cover for you. Give me until tomorrow, and you'll need to just show them the basic day to day reports and things you do, so we don't get behind."

"Alright, that's great. I'll do that."

"Sounds good. Just touch base, so I know when you're coming back."

"I will. Thanks again."

"Sure, and good luck!"

Chapter Seventeen

Michael and Sarah's drive to New York took several days, over stretches of highway that sprawled out in long lines. Plenty of things captured their attention, like billboards and the occasional goofy bumper sticker. At the bare minimum, they filled the silences with Michael's MP3 player.

During the long hours behind the while, Michael thought about his situation at home. Thinking about the way he left things at Tech 4 U worried him.

His mom wasn't well either, and he dreaded a call from his dad about her while he was away. It seemed though, for the first time, his dad thought of him as an adult. Michael dwelled on how good it felt when he stood his ground.

When the fear about his future crept in, he reminded himself he made the right move with this trip. He just needed that nagging voice of doubt quieted.

Michael's GPS came to life, and announced the next highway exit. "So, whatcha thinking about?" asked Sarah.

"Women always wanna know what men are thinking. Why's that?"

"Just making conversation, crabby. C'mon, it's a long way to the Big Apple."

"Uh, thinking about what I'm doing. You know, for a job. I mean, Tech 4 U is out, and I don't know what that wreck's gonna do to the limo business. But hey, my friend needs help."

"I appreciate that, and thanks for putting up some money. Hope you get to see Charlotte."

"We'll see."

Michael admitted to himself that Sarah was fun to be around, and she looked great, even in the T-shirts and jeans she wore at Ales.

In fact, she always looked good to him. Especially when they-

Ok. Enough. He had her as a captive audience. It was time. What's the worst that could have happened?

Her elbow in his groin, before she took his car, and he hitchhiked home? Naah she was tougher than that. She's handled worse than a little Q&A.

"While we're just talking," Michael said, "Was wondering if you ever thought about that night."

Long pause.

"Oh, you mean the night you and I hooked up?"

Michael caught her smirk as she twisted her fingers around. "Yeah. I mean, we never really talked about it."

She turned to him. "It was more than a little complicated, if you recall."

"Yeah, you wanted to get back at Jimmy for cheating on you, and I was available."

"I was 16, I was mad as hell and yeah, I wanted to get back at him."

"And I helped you out."

"Don't make it sound like you didn't enjoy it," Sarah chuckled.

"You kidding? It was... yeah. Well, ever wonder what it'd be like?"

"What 'what' would be like?"

"You and me. A couple."

Sarah sighed, and played with her hair. "Yeah, I guess. I dunno. You're really sweet, but I dunno Michael. You aren't very focused."

"Huh?"

"Honey, you bounce around a lot in jobs, and whatever your latest fixation is. Now it's Charlotte. A few months ago she didn't even exist, and now you're all over her. It's like you're always shooting yourself in the foot, second guessing what you're doing after you start something."

"So maybe I don't have it together yet."

"I noticed. Don't worry, I'm not much further along."

His hands gripped the wheel tighter. "I just don't want to end up like that guy Brad I've been rooming with. He goes out almost every night, gets out of his head loaded or who knows what else, then crashes and goes to work, mostly on time. I mean, sure I've done that too. But he's almost 40. Scraping by, no wife and kids, no real career other than whatever job he can hang onto. Just seems sad. I mean, do you really know where you're going?"

"I have an idea."

"Yeah, well what then?"

"My boys safe and cared for. Me having a better job, paralegal or something maybe. No more radio, no more Ales."

"What about a partner? See that in your picture?"

She chuckled. "Haven't been able to nail that one down, no pun intended. Plenty of Mr. He'll-Do-For-Now's out there so far."

"Well don't cancel out all your options out of spite," he said. Sarah glanced at him for a few moments while she debated her reply, but decided against it and slumped back in her seat.

As they drove on a few miles in silence, Michael busied his mind by thoughts of Charlotte.

He imagined a location set for Stewardesses on a street in New York City. Charlotte would be there with fellow cast members acting out a scene. A barricade would prevent Michael from getting any closer than two hundred feet. That would be close enough, however. Charlotte and the others, dressed in classy 1960s attire, would run through several takes of the scene.

After an hour of filming, the director would call a wrap for the day. The crew would begin to break down the lighting and camera gear. The cast would linger with the crowd, taking pictures and signing autographs. As Charlotte was one of the more popular cast members, the crowd around her would be larger than the

*others. This, of course, would be no deterrent for Michael, who'd
wait his turn, camera in hand and huge smile on his face.*

*After awhile, Charlotte would begin to work her way through
the crowd, getting closer to him. His nervous energy would build
as she approached. Finally...her in the flesh. She'd look directly at
Michael and say, "Hello there!" Her soft Canadian accent would
linger in the air as Michael fumbled to reply, "Uh, hi!"*

*Giggling softly, Charlotte would reply, "Would you like to take
a picture of me or one of us together?"*

Quickly, Michael responds with, "Oh us together, please!"

*Smiling, Charlotte nods and stands alongside Michael as he
hands his camera to a fellow fan. Once the fan stood back a few
feet, Charlotte places an arm around Michael's back, and he feels
a pang of butterflies. "You've no idea what this means to me," he'd
say, his voice shaking with excitement.*

*Laughing, Charlotte would say, "Aww, you're so sweet. Thank
you so much for your support."*

"It's so much fun to watch you."

"And people like you allow me to do the work that I love!"

Michael thought, *At least that's what I HOPE would happen. I
just don't want to babble.* He hoped he wouldn't have used the star-
struck approach, but this was the biggest celebrity he'd meet in
person yet, so he didn't know how he'd react until the time came.

Sarah stretched in her seat. "Let me know when you want me
to drive, okay?"

"Yep. So what do you think of Ashlyn?"

Sarah shrugged. "She doesn't like me very much."

"What makes you say that?"

"I'm a woman, Michael. We know these things."

"Oh I see. Seems cool to me."

"Yeah, decent enough. Bit more outgoing than Jack. Come to
think of it, Jack always was more on the milder side. When we
dated, he wasn't really mingling much at parties and dances.
Maybe he just needed the right person to bring it out in him."

Michael glanced at Sarah. "Ever think about him like that?"

"Hmm. I guess not. It's been so long, you know? We've been
just friends for awhile. It's like that bit that existed between us
never resolved. Just kind of fizzled out. There wasn't a big break

off moment where I threw his crap in the yard and called the cops or something."

"Well good thing for that."

Sarah turned to look at Michael. "Hey, thanks again for doing this trip. It's really sweet of you. I know my car would've never have made it."

"No worries, dear."

"I feel bad about you losing your job for this."

"Yeah, that wasn't great."

"I mean, what're you gonna do about that?"

"Not sure. Maybe I can pick up some time at B&G again. Or Ales?"

Sarah chuckled. "You waiting tables?"

"Hey, who knows? Anyway, happy to help you and Kelly. You're right, your Nissan wouldn't have made it, much as that thing burns oil. Besides, I'm getting a little something extra out of this."

Sarah laughed. "Oh yes, your love, Charlotte. How could I forget? You two going to run off when you meet, and make the short run of *Stewardesses* even shorter?"

"Hey, come on. I like her. She's talented, and they have great storylines about her."

"Oh cut the shit, Michael. You want her body."

Michael glanced at Sarah. "What?? Okay, well sure I'd like a shot at that. I'm a guy, I notice these things. What can I do?"

Sarah turned more towards Michael in her seat, intrigued by his argument. "Okay, so what exactly is it about her? Why are you so taken with this woman?"

Michael paused. He hadn't been put on the spot like this about his fan worship of Charlotte before. Further, he hadn't been called out by someone like Sarah on his interest in Charlotte.

They drove on in silence for a minute or two. Michael struggled to come up with an answer. Sarah looked back to the road, and grinned slightly. She was always fond of how she teased Michael, but this time she felt more of a tinge of wonder and hurt.

Michael took a deep breath. "Sarah, all I can say is... I've been single for awhile, as you know. And yes, I do enjoy a lot about being on my own. But I miss some things, like having someone around who's with me. You know, 'with me'? Not having to worry about feeling weird at a movie because I'm going in to watch alone. Being able to go out to a restaurant with a date or just stay at home with someone. Things like that."

"Yeah, but you also need to realize how nice being a single person with no kids can be, Michael. Look at me. My two boys are my life, but they are my life. I love them and never regret having them, but I'm alone. It's not easy for a single mom with two boys to convince someone to be a fixture in their life, and deal with her schedule, cancellations, and things like that."

Michael glanced at Sarah. "Yeah, I guess. Ever think about just taking a chance out there, romantically?"

"Sure. It isn't easy for me though. I'm still kind of in my own realm, playing mama bear, protector of my world with my two baby cubs. It's like I have things under control now, and bringing someone else in disrupts that."

"Right, you and your boys have been through enough."

"Yep. So let's get back to you and your fixation on Charlotte. You say you're feeling the pangs of being single and alone. What's it about a fictional character that makes your real life situation more tolerable?"

"She's a friendly, pretty face I can always count on to be around?"

"Yeah, but she's on TV, it's not like she's on your sofa, feeding you grapes."

"No, but it feels like I'm less alone when I watch her on TV."

Sarah was perplexed. "Alright. But then how does pining for an actress on *Stewardesses* help you feel better in real life?"

Michael shrugged. "I like focusing on someone. You've seen the show. Monique's beautiful, and confident and real. She isn't perfect either. She makes mistakes. She slept with a married man from one of her flights, and she has a habit of loving the wrong people. But she keeps trying. Maybe I saw a little bit of hope for me through her. Kind of like 'If she can pull herself up out of being knocked down, maybe I can too.'"

He continued, "I used to see these people coming into B&G buying groceries for big meals, and I envied them. Know why? Because I knew they were buying to feed a family."

Sarah glanced back at him. "Your parents, Michael, are your

family. You lived with them until very recently, right? And you can visit anytime."

"Yeah, but that's not what I'm talking about. Look, you have your boys. Jack has Ashlyn. Yes, I have my parents, but I've had that since birth. What's next? I want to progress, I need something more. I don't want to just live in this rut I've been stuck in."

Sarah touched Michael's arm. "Hey, it's okay. I know it's frustrating. Just – all I'm going to say about that is be careful with those feelings. Don't let feelings of loneliness lead to desperation. If you're not careful, you may find yourself doing some stupid things and getting stuck in a situation you don't want. That's how I became an unwed teen mom of two. Don't get me wrong, my two boys are my life, and I wouldn't trade them. But it's been a hard road for me. Mom helped, but I've had to give up a lot too."

Michael nodded. "Yeah, I guess. I'll be careful. Hey, we need to fill up. How about you take the wheel? Another two hours and we can find a hotel."

"Sounds good. I'll call ahead about Kelly's hospital."

***

They'd been back on the highway maybe ten minutes when it happened.

"Not again," Michael said.

"What?"

"The check engine light's on."

"Wait... again? It happened already? I missed it."

"No, no, happened to me on the town car."

Sarah chuckled. "You're kidding, right?"

"Wish the hell I was."

Just then, a whining noise joined their conversation.

"Now what?" Sarah asked.

"I don't know, I can fill 'em with gas and drive 'em. That's about where it ends."

"Well damn, maybe we just chance it?"

Michael glanced at her. "I dunno. Last time this happened, it was the radiator, and we don't want to be on the highway if that goes out."

Sarah checked Michael's GPS. "There wasn't anything at that podunk stop we just made except for a gas station and a greasy spoon. Knoxville is about five miles up. Why don't we try for there?"

"Guess that'll do."

***

They puttered into a car shop in Knoxville. Their worries came down to a slipped alternator belt and some bad spark plugs. It was late in the day, so they were told it would be ready sometime next morning.

Between the hassle in general and the wait at the shop, they were both a little too wiped to get back on the road anyway. They decided on a hotel down the street from the car shop. Not exactly a four star establishment, but they were on a budget. It would have to do. They were able to get a room with two double beds.

After a meal of sandwiches, chips and soft drinks from the nearest highway gas station convenience store, they sat down, each on a bed and turned the TV on. It was almost 8pm.

Sarah stretched out on her bed, and sighed. "I checked in with mom on the boys."

"How are things on the home front?"

"Typical. Mom said they're being good for the most part, but occasionally they fight over some toy or something."

"Sibling rivalry, what can you do?"

"True."

"What about Kelly?"

"Called her while you were booking the room. Resting and okay right now."

"That's a relief."

They both froze for a moment as a "Coming up next" promo for *Stewardesses* appeared on the TV. Michael smiled. "Well what do you know about that?"

"Their last attempt to try and bump up the audience?"

"Yeah, or they're just getting all the blood out of them while the shows are new."

"Gonna miss the pretty pilots." Sarah sighed.

"What a damn shame if they let it die." Michael quipped. "Oh sure, let's get rid of the shows with thought out story lines and interesting characters for more reality junk."

Sarah faced Michael. She grabbed a pillow from her bed and hugged it while she lay on her side. "So... on the subject of 'reality junk', we were talking earlier about why you're so into *Stewardesses*."

Michael glanced at Sarah. "Yeah? I thought we covered that."

"Well, not entirely. I understand you're focusing on this woman because she is 'real' to you. But come on, Michael. Don't you ever think about getting out there and actually being with someone?"

Michael shifted a bit. He looked at Sarah for a moment. "Well, yeah. I've dated, I've had sex with girls and all. Just nothing seemed to take. There's a missing connection usually. I'm often waiting for the other shoe to drop. I usually relate to girls on one thing or another. For example, the sex is great, but we don't have much in common; or we don't really mesh physically, but we have the best time talking and have a lot in common."

Michael stared at the TV for a moment. Then, he caught Sarah's gaze, as she studied him closely. He continued, "After awhile, we fall into a pattern of just maintaining, treading water so to speak. And then comes the inevitable moment where one of us, usually the girl but sometimes myself, gets fed up with the lack of direction, and it ends. And I hate endings in relationships. It's usually unpleasant at best and very painful at worst. I just hate losing things. It feels like a waste, kind of like what I'm going through with working one dead end job to the next instead of having a career."

"Well what's the alternative, then? Not trying at all?"

"I don't know."

"You did just ask if I thought about us being together."

"Well yeah, but you didn't seem to be chomping at the bit at the idea." Michael chuckled.

"Trying to be careful about bringing you into that world, dear. Remember, I've got a crew."

"How do you handle kids and dating?"

"Ha! Well as you may have noticed, I haven't been concerned

145

with dating much, lately anyway. My schedule keeps me pretty busy. I admit, I miss having another adult around, like a relationship. I'm so damn alone all the time."

Michael watched her intently. She continued, "Alright, fine. Yeah I thought about what you said. Us being together. Here and there anyway."

She turned to him again. "Oh don't give me that smirk. You started this whole conversation on the road."

"What, I was just saying-"

"I've had enough bad turns for awhile, Michael. No offense, but jumping from guy to guy hasn't gone great overall in case you hadn't noticed."

Michael turned the TV off. "I'm not just some guy."

Sarah sighed. "You're not. You're incredibly sweet. But what if it doesn't work out? I lose one of my closest friends in the process?"

He sat on the side of her bed. "I can't say if it will or won't. But neither can you."

Sarah sighed, and ruffled her hair as Michael continued, "Look, I've been taking a lot of chances over the years. Yeah, lot of them ended up shitty. My own parents had enough, and kicked me out. Now I'm unemployed to boot. I- don't know where I'll be next month."

"Will you cut back on the dramatic wailings? Dammit Michael, see this is what I'm talking about. You have no kids, but you're starting a business. That's huge. You're heading somewhere, you just need to realize it."

"You admitted to thinking about it."

"Yeah, well so what?"

"Let's try it."

She glanced at the clock. "It's getting late."

"Not too late... yet." He climbed up on her bed, and before she knew what happened, they kissed. Soft and slowly. Their lips warmly caressed. Her eyes widened at first, then gently closed as she let forth a soft moan.

"Well that was nice." He sighed, a smile on his lips.

"Yeah, well. You always did know how to kiss a girl."

"Do I need to stop?"

Her eyes closed, savoring his closeness to her. Feelings dormant for many years began to bubble to the surface. "No. I'm... it's okay."

Michael reached for the light as she began to undress. They fell into each other's arms, and awakened old feelings. Caring, passion, lust, all intertwined.

As they lay awake in the afterglow, no words passed between them. They caressed and nuzzled each other's warmth. Their eyes peered into the blackness of the room, starting into something. A future, maybe? As Michael's thoughts diverted toward Sarah, she felt a lone tear roll down her cheek. Her mind was mulling over a single thought: *What now? Is Jimmy truly behind me? Can I finally move on? And should it be with Michael?*

***

The car fixed, they pressed onto New York and made it up on Wednesday. Their funds only allowed them to stay a few days, so they had to move fast. They found out that Kelly was at the Vassar Brothers Medical Center in Poughkeepsie, NY. They found a room at a Holiday Inn Express and checked in.

When they settled in, Sarah called the hospital to get directions. Michael fired up his laptop to see what he could find about the *Stewardesses* filming locations. They were about 90 minutes from the usual filming locations for *Stewardesses* in Manhattan.

Michael logged into Twitter briefly as @Tim707.

@Tim707: Hello from upstate New York! Writer is visiting a sick friend.

He checked online and saw a few tweets from Monique characters. A minute or two, his tweet received a reply.

@Beaute707: @Tim707 "Welcome, mon amour, to town! // I hope your friend is okay! *hugs*

Michael smiled at the greeting and well wishes. He glanced at Sarah. She was still on the phone and wrote rather furiously on the pad of paper provided for the room by the hotel.

Michael logged into Facebook to see who was online. He noticed Jack logged in, and sent him a quick message.

Hey dude! Sarah and I made it to NY! Waiting to figure out when we can go visit Kelly and see *Stewardesses* filming.

As he sent the message to Jack, Sarah hung up the phone. She looked over the notes she had written for a few moments. "So here's the deal. She's probably gonna be released in a few days. Still waiting to hear back from the Culinary Institute of America about her enrollment status. But she sounds good, and is anxious to see us."

Michael nodded. "Okay, so it's almost lunchtime, how about we grab a bite, and go up to see her afterward?"

"Sounds good to me."

Chapter Eighteen

After lunch at a local deli, they got back into Michael's car and headed for Vassar Brothers Medical Center. Kelly lay in bed, covered with a bed sheet. A lone IV for fluids and medication was still in her arm, but she looked fairly calm and alert. She smiled as Sarah and Michael entered her room.

"Hey little sis! So good to see you!" Kelly extended her arms to Sarah.

Sarah smiled as she hugged Kelly. As she replied, "You too," her voice quavered a bit. The sight of Kelly in such shape made it near impossible for Sarah's stoic facade, though she tried her best.

They embraced as Michael stood back a bit. Kelly closed her eyes and sighed. "It's okay. I'm going to be alright. They wanted to keep an eye on me for a few days." Sarah sniffled as she stood back up from their embrace. Michael grabbed one of the chairs in the room and brought it to Sarah. Kelly smiled at him, "Hello Michael. Long time."

"Hi Kelly, yes it has been. Glad you're better."

"Thanks."

Sarah sat down in her chair and gently grasped Kelly's arm.

"Do they know what caused the seizures?"

"No, but I'll be on anti-seizure medications for a few months. They want me to follow up a few times to make sure all's well. Oh yeah, I can't drive until I'm cleared."

"Well, there's public transportation, right?"

"Yep, could be worse. Ooh, maybe I shouldn't say that out loud." All three chuckled.

Kelly continued. "I'm not sure what all this does to my enrollment. So far, I'm still on financial aid, so I can stay up here between semesters with the catering jobs I've been able to pick up here and there. But now, all of that's up in the air."

Sarah nodded. "When can you find out more?"

"I'm supposed to call first thing tomorrow, and see where I stand. We'll see. So, what have I been missing in Metairie? How are my two favorite nephews?"

Sarah laughed, "Oh, getting into trouble and raising holy hell."

"Of course."

"Actually, they're doing pretty well. I'm the queen of homework with them. We have our little routine, and they're handling things alright. Mom is keeping an eye on them while I'm away."

"Yeah, she said when she called a few days ago. That's great. How about work?"

"Oh, balancing two jobs is a chore in and of itself. WZEB-FM pays the bills, and if my boss Peter would let me breathe every once in awhile, wouldn't be so bad. If I didn't know better I'd say he had a crush on me."

Michael was taken aback by Sarah's comment on her boss. "A crush?"

Sarah quickly glanced at Michael. "Huh? Oh, it's nothing. He's just an ass."

Michael slowly nodded, but mentally chewed a bit on this idea of Sarah and Peter, and what exactly they were to each other. Michael wondered if Sarah was lying to him about Peter.

Kelly said, "And what about that bar. Ales, right?"

"Yes, Ales is still rolling along. I'm not a millionaire, but I'm hoping you'll make that big splash on the restaurant scene, and help your little sister out one day." Sarah giggled as she playfully tugged Kelly's arm.

Kelly in turn laughed. "Who knows? And Michael, what have you been up to?"

Michael was jarred from his consternation about Sarah and Peter by Kelly's sudden question. "Me? Well, I just left a job at an electronics store to help Sarah make it here. That's pretty much it for right now."

Kelly nodded. "Wow, that's really nice. Sorry about that though."

Michael shrugged. "Didn't want Sarah making her way up here alone."

Sarah placed her hand on Michael's shoulder, and interjected, "And he's pining for a TV actress who happens to be in New York right now doing location shoots."

Michael shrugged off Sarah's arm. "Hey, you're watching it too. Didn't see you change the channel the other night."

Kelly laughed. "You two. Well I can't say I blame you for being hooked on a TV series. I watch a few here and there. I know several film in New York. Which one are you guys talking about?"

"*Stewardesses*," Michael and Sarah replied in unison.

Kelly smiled, "Oh right, the 1960's airline drama. Michael, got a thing for sexy women in uniform?"

Michael laughed, "What is this, I'm getting double teamed here? Yeah, I have a thing for hot chicks on a plane. Sue me."

They laughed again. Kelly said, "Thanks for coming up here, you guys. This means so much."

Sarah stood up and gently placed her hand on Kelly's shoulder. "I wanted to make sure you're okay, sis. I took a week off WZEB, and Ales is hanging on to my spot for now. We'll manage."

When a nurse entered the room to take some vital signs from Kelly, Michael and Sarah left for the day.

***

Back at their hotel room that evening, they wound down for the night. Sarah brushed her teeth. Her back was to Michael as he sat on the bed with his laptop. He looked toward her. "So, what's with you and Peter?"

Sarah stopped. She rinsed and glanced at Michael in the mirror. "Me and Peter?"

"Yeah. He's got a thing for you?"

"No, I said, 'If I didn't know any better I'd think he has a crush on me.' Why?"

Michael shrugged. "Just kinda surprised me."

"Well, I don't think that's it, but the way he lays into me sometimes, I'm wondering if there's something else going on."

Michael nodded. Sarah continued brushing her teeth. She'd just begun to wonder where Peter's treatment of her came from, and now Michael had started to wonder about it as well. Boys, always complicated, she mused and smirked to herself in the mirror.

They didn't hear from Kelly until late Monday morning. Sarah answered the call. Kelly was noticeably agitated.

"They really did it."

"Who did what?"

"My school. Seems they didn't care for me dropping out mid semester very much. Some bullshit about a waiting list or something. I won't be cleared by the doctor for school or anything until they evaluate me in a few months. I need to reapply to the school to continue on, which means I'm out for another semester, maybe longer."

"Oh no. What about your financial aid?"

Kelly sniffled a bit. "In limbo. I have two weeks to move out of my place. What am I going to do?"

Sarah glanced at Michael. He was still engrossed with his laptop. She thought for a moment. "Kelly, we'll figure this out. Do you have any money?"

"I've got some in savings, maybe a few hundred dollars."

"Okay. Any idea when you'll get out of the hospital?"

"Today, tomorrow at the latest."

"Alright. We're just going to have to help you move. You come back to Metairie. I'm sure Mom wouldn't mind putting you up for a few weeks while this mess gets sorted out."

"I hate having to ask her for help though."

"Now you sound like me. Look, this is a rough situation. You can't drive. You're not going to be in school for several months, and I know you can't afford to live here on your own. Sometimes you need to do what's necessary to take care of yourself."

"You're right, sis."

"Sometimes."

"Thanks for all you're doing. I love you."

"Love you too." Sarah hung the phone up.

Chapter Nineteen

Michael glanced up to see Sarah's concerned expression.

"Kelly has to move back?"

"Yeah. Her school gave some crap excuse about not wanting to waste a spot when they have such a big waiting list. And she loses her financial aid if she isn't enrolled. So she can't stay here."

Michael glanced at his laptop. On the screen at the moment was the "On Location" announcement for the current week for *Stewardesses* on the Facebook page. He looked back to Sarah.

Sarah walked toward Michael. She placed her hands on the back of another chair at the table. She sighed and glanced down for a moment. "I need to help her move."

Michael was taken aback. He leaned back in his chair. "Right. You... we came to help."

"She has some money, probably enough to rent a van to move her things. She can't drive either, so she's going to need help."

"How much time?"

"We can't wait too long, still have a few days drive ahead of us, and I can't keep my jobs on hold or I'll really be messed up."

Michael nudged the laptop away. "So this needs to happen like now."

"Pretty much."

Michael was stunned. His original plan was in jeopardy. For the first time, a jolting thought pervaded his mind: *This girl needs you, Michael. Her sister is in bad shape. She needs someone to help her move her things out of town, or she will be evicted.*

His glance wavered back to the screen, showing the pictures of the *Stewardesses* actresses and the fans posing for pictures with them. *I'm so close,* he thought. *This show may very well be canceled, and I won't have this chance again.*

But it's Sarah. You know, the girl you can't get out of your head? Oh... and the REAL girl, who's been there for you since high school? Not some actress or other fantasy.

Michael looked into Sarah's eyes. He knew he had a task way more important than some TV actress, or anything else for that matter. Kelly needed Sarah, and Sarah needed him.

His focus became crystalline. "Let's do it, we'll rent a van and get going."

Sarah's eyes widened. "But you're gonna miss your chance to catch her... why you came here."

Michael softly closed his laptop. He took a slow breath, and shook his head. "You... are why I'm here." He stood up.

A few tears rolled down Sarah's cheeks, she reached for Michael. "Sorry you missed out."

They hugged, and Michael chuckled softly. "I didn't miss out. Let's get this done."

***

Kelly's apartment was a dormitory style building adjacent to the cooking school. Her unit was on the fifth floor. It was more or less an efficiency apartment. Kelly had a bed, sofa, desk, and several moderate sized pieces of furniture, as well as a few other small items.

Michael took a gaze around the room. "We're gonna need a truck for all this stuff."

Kelly said, "It's okay, I can cover it. Maybe a U-Haul or something?"

Michael nodded. "Yeah, but you can't drive. Alright, let's do this. We just need to find the nearest U-Haul, rent a truck and start loading it. I'll drive it. You and Sarah take my car, and we convoy back home to Metairie."

"You sure about that, Michael? Ever drive a truck?" Kelly asked.

Michael's mind flashed back to the wreck. Was he ready? He'd made the trip up there, but he never drove a big truck before.

"No, but how hard can it be? Hiring movers costs a lot more, and we'd be stuck waiting for them. It's gonna be fine." He smiled.

Kelly and Sarah glanced at each other, then nodded in agreement. Michael felt good about the plan. He caught Sarah's proud glance of him. It felt good, but more so he felt great about his feeling of direction.

While Kelly called U-Haul, Michael and Sarah pulled items out of their respective places, and arranged them in a line near the door. Sarah commented, "Thanks again for this. I know you wanted to catch that live *Stewardesses* shoot."

Michael paused as he heard Sarah's words. He felt a slight twinge of regret, in that he came so close. Any glimmer of regret was squashed when he saw the look of gratitude in Sarah's eyes.

"Sure. It's alright. This is the... right thing to do."

Sarah smiled. She turned back to picking up items. "Gotta say, this trip's turning out way more interesting than I ever thought."

The three of them took a break to drive to U-Haul to pick up the truck. Kelly signed the papers, and the three of them returned to pack Kelly's items up for the trip back to Metairie.

***

While Kelly and Sarah worked upstairs, Michael spread blankets in the back of the truck for the furniture.

The truck was parked at the edge of the parking lot. While he opened packs of blankets, Michael glanced across the street. A tree lined sidewalk separated the street from a row of brownstone apartment buildings. Several people strolled along beneath the trees across from Michael. It looked how what he imagined a New

York residential area would look: part urban edifice, but with a little charm from the greenery around. Pretty much their version of the Garden District back in New Orleans.

A few minutes in the back of the truck, and it was all set for the furniture and boxes. Michael slid out the back, and took another glance at the picturesque scene across from him when he was distracted by a flash of color.

Not just any color. It was blue. Wait, a woman in uniform? He walked a bit closer to the street. It was a stewardess uniform. She looked like she was studying a piece of paper in her hand. She walked close to the street, and the sun caught her between two of the trees. She swept the hair from her face and glanced around. The brown hair. That smile. Was it her?

He froze for a moment. Was he dreaming again? Cars zoomed past on the street. He stopped a minute. He realized he wasn't in the 60s, and also not on a plane.

Michael heard Sarah behind him. "Hey, we're about ready to move boxes. You coming?"

"Yeah in a second - you seeing this?"

Sarah stood alongside him. "Hey, is that Charlotte?"

"I think so. So you see her too?"

Sarah elbowed him. "Um, yeah!"

"What the hell is she doing here? Don't see any crews around."

"Well maybe she lives here. You gonna go talk to her or what?" She laughed.

Michael smiled at Sarah. "You're coming too."

Kelly joined them, a small box under one arm. "All set to start. What are y'all looking at?"

Michael grabbed the box from Kelly. "You been holding out on us, Kelly? All this time you lived across the street from Charlotte Ducrest?"

Kelly shrugged. "Oh that's her? Wow, guess we passed each other up, different schedules. Go catch her, we have a few minutes."

Sarah and Michael crossed over as Charlotte still studied the paper she held.

"Excuse me," Michael asked. "Are you-"

She looked up, an annoyed expression on her face. "Hmm?

Oh, I don't suppose either of you know the quickest way to get to Riverfront Park. I'm late."

"Um, I'm sorry. We're both really big fans of you and *Stewardesses* and well, just wanted to say thanks for being so great."

Her expression faded to a faint smile. "Well thank you very much." She glanced back at the paper, some kind of city map.

"Shame what happened to the show." Michael offered.

Charlotte glanced back at Michael, her face registered he wasn't just a passing fan. "Oh yes, well at least we can finish the last two."

"I'm Michael, by the way. This is my friend, Sarah."

"Nice to meet you both."

"He has a crush on you," Sarah chided.

Michael eyed Sarah as Charlotte managed a smile. "I really do need to catch a cab." She waved toward a cab as it zoomed past them.

"Wait! Maybe we can take you there," Michael blurted out. Sarah leaned over to whisper, "We've been here for all of two days, you have no idea where you're going, and your GPS has crapped out."

"Kelly," Michael whispered back.

"P.S. we also have a little move going on, remember?"

"Got an idea," Michael replied, his eyes beamed.

"And what if Kelly doesn't know where this place is?"

"We'll see."

Charlotte turned back to them. "I couldn't impose like that. I'll figure something out."

"It's no trouble. Really. Our friend lives across the street from you, she can get you there faster than waiting for a cab."

Michael waved across the street to Kelly who watched them. She waved back slowly.

Charlotte sighed and said, "Okay, well let's get going."

***

Michael's car careened through the streets of Hyde Park, as Kelly gave directions from the passenger seat.

"Okay, better take a right here, otherwise we'll catch the light ahead and it's long." Kelly advised.

"Right," Michael replied. He glanced back in the rear view for a moment. "All good back there?"

"Doing fine," Sarah commented. Charlotte gazed out the window, but nodded in response.

"So, you miss Canada?" Michael asked.

"I do, but it's not much to visit from here. Of course, being out of work soon I'll be auditioning a lot, and who knows where my next gig will be."

"You must have a crazy social life," Sarah said. "I mean, I guess you have lots of opportunities there?"

Michael caught a glimpse of Charlotte as she pondered the question, while she gazed outside again. "Not what you might think. I don't have much time to be with someone. I mean, it kind of suits me. I like independence." She gazed off, and bit her lip. She appeared lost in thought.

"Had you checked out the Facebook page on *Stewardesses* at all?" Michael asked.

Charlotte replied, "Oh yes, it's lovely. It's nice seeing all those people sharing what they like with their friends and family. Feels like a home."

"Yeah, I'm around that page every week, with Sarah here and our other friend Jack." Michael said.

"How nice. You two, you must be dating?"

Michael froze. Silence in the car for a few minutes, broken up when Sarah and Kelly giggled. "Well, I wouldn't go that far," Sarah remarked, and patted Michael's shoulder. "But he does seem to like me." Charlotte smiled.

Flushed a bit, Michael collected himself. "Yeah, well she's great. She..." He glanced back in the mirror and saw Charlotte chuckling and Sarah smiling, with a twinkle in her eye.

What?

He didn't feel mocked this time. Her gaze was more inviting than that.

What am I doing? I'm driving a car with some actress I had a one in a million chance of meeting, and right next to her is this girl who has been in front of me the whole time.

A siren jolted Michael out of his thoughts. A police car and its lights filled up the rear view mirror. "Oh great." He pulled the car over.

Kelly said, "And we're very close to the park now."

Charlotte replied, "Really? Maybe I should just walk from here."

"Um, I'd wait until the cop is done," Sarah cautioned.

Michael got a ticket for speeding, and he decided against the "Chauffeuring an actress to a TV shoot" excuse. As the cop pulled away, Charlotte let herself out. "Well, thank you all for an interesting ride. And I'm only ten minutes late."

"Sorry about that," Michael said.

Shrugging, she replied, "It's okay. On my track record, it isn't my worst." She regarded them and smiled. Her hands pointed at Michael and Sarah, she commented, "Don't miss out on having someone you connect with." Smiling, she waved and walked off.

They watched her go for a minute. "She was pretty nice," Kelly remarked.

"Yeah, and insightful," Michael said.

"Mmhmm. Lots of ideas in one car ride," Sarah mused.

Michael eased the car back into traffic. "Thanks for the detour, Kelly. Owe you."

"I'd say we're even. But when we're back home, tell me more about that deal you mentioned, alright?"

***

The threesome scoured Kelly's small apartment. Sarah reviewed the scene for a moment as they loaded boxes. "Kelly, I'm glad you know how to pack light." Sarah laughed. "I never did get that. I pack three days worth of clothes for an overnight trip."

"Oh, yeah, sis, I remember. And this was before your boys too. Michael, you should see how much she packed when we went to the water park outside of Baton Rouge one time."

Michael smiled. "Ha! I went to the beach for Spring Break with her and some friends during high school. The words 'steamer trunk' come to mind."

Sarah smirked at them both, and extended her middle finger as

160

she continued on the boxes and lined them up by the door.

The U-Haul was a 16 foot truck, and everything fit with a little room to spare. After some help with the bigger pieces of furniture from a few neighbors in the building, the truck was closed up and locked. The three of them stood on the street and looked at Kelly's former residence.

"I never thought this would happen to me," Kelly sighed.

Sarah placed an arm around her shoulder. "Gonna be alright, sis. You just need to regroup, that's all."

Kelly shrugged. Sarah patted her shoulder, and added, "You'll be back here before you know it. You have that fire in you, and I bet this is just gonna stoke that fire even more. I feel sorry for these jokers once you get back." Kelly laughed at Sarah's reassuring words.

Michael fished the keys to his car out of his pocket. He extended them to Sarah, and quipped, "Take it easy on the road, daredevil."

Sarah laughed. "Yeah, you too, big trucker man."

"Just be careful."

"Oh come on, you think I'd endanger my sister's life like that? We have some prime catch up time now anyway."

Michael smiled. "Okay, that sounds good. Why don't you guys lead the way and I'll follow."

Chapter Twenty

They set out on the road to return to Metairie. Once they made it through the chaotic New York traffic and onto the highway, the long drive ahead gave way to conversation. As Sarah drove, Kelly reclined a bit in her seat.

"Nice of Michael to help," Kelly commented.

"He got what he wanted," Sarah smirked.

"Huh?"

"That actress we drove? He's had it bad for her for a few months now. Think that little car ride about made his year."

"Ah, right."

Sarah bit her lip in thought as Kelly gazed out at the road. "He's a great guy."

"You like him."

Sarah flashed Kelly an incredulous look. "What? No. I mean, he's really sweet and all, but not like that."

"Sarah, don't bullshit me. You're my baby sis. I know you. You like this guy. I remember those weekends when you were in high school, and I was at UNO. Friday nights, Jack and Michael would be around the house waiting for you to get ready."

"Yeah, and I was dating Jack then."

"I know, I know. But I remember a few times you giving Michael advice or something. Both of you, talking and laughing together. Like you had your own inside jokes or something."

Sarah chuckled. "Okay, maybe we kinda had a connection."

"Yeah, more than kinda," Kelly giggled.

"I dunno. He's special. But I'm not on the straight and narrow. Remember what Jimmy did to me? Michael's great, but I won't risk losing him."

"Great guy, and he came with you to help."

"I don't need another baby daddy that won't be around." Sarah sighed.

"Just do yourself a favor, and think about it. Never know how it might be."

Sarah's cell phone rang. Kelly answered and heard Michael on the other end. "How's the convoy holding up?" He asked.

Kelly glanced back to see the U-Haul truck behind them. "Doing well I guess. How about you and Big Bertha back there?"

"Not bad. Hey, y'all hungry? Coulda eaten twenty minutes ago."

"Let's see. Hang on." Kelly turned to Sarah, "You want to get a bite? Michael's hungry."

Sarah kept her eyes on the road but smirked. "Sure, sounds good to me. Next exit."

Kelly returned to the phone, "It's a plan. Follow us."

Chapter Twenty-one

They stopped in New Jersey at a place called Gayle's Diner, near the highway. Gayle's Diner was a typical road stop restaurant. The building looked to be at least forty years old, probably one of the first built in the area. It was surrounded by several gas stations and a few fast-food chains. Michael and Sarah had been eating too much fast food. Kelly was glad to not be eating hospital food for a change. All three wanted a meal with a little more substance to it. They walked into the restaurant and sat at a table. The interior of Gayle's Diner looked like it hadn't changed a whole lot during the history of the establishment. Yellowed drapes dangled over the windows, probably original decor. The table was made of wood and metal and felt like it came from someone's kitchen. The air had a prevalent odor of grease, fried meat and onions.

A waitress walked up to their table, handed out menus and said, "Good afternoon, welcome to Gayle's. Would y'all like something to drink while you look through the menu?"

Michael nodded and replied, "I'll have a lemonade."

"Tea," Sarah chirped.

"Coke for me," said Kelly.

The waitress nodded and left to get their drink order as they checked out the menu. Written on the back of its front was a brief history of the diner, followed by a list of their signature menu items. As he read the menu, they heard some laughter nearby. They looked around to see their waitress with an older gentleman at another table. The man looked to be in his eighties, and Michael wouldn't have paid much attention to him if he hadn't noticed a laptop and a lady's hat resting on the man's table.

Michael nodded to the man and asked the girls, "Wonder what his deal is?"

"Big outing of the week?" Sarah remarked.

Kelly frowned slightly. "No telling. Looks nice enough though. Maybe he's just lonely."

They returned their attention to their menus. More laughter came from the other table. Their waitress kissed the man on the cheek, and went to the kitchen area. Moments later, she returned with their drinks. "Would y'all like to hear our specials, or are you ready?"

Michael closed the menu and replied, "I'm ready." He leaned toward her. "Who's that guy over there?"

The waitress glanced back toward the gentleman and said, "Oh, that's Mr. Costel."

"Looks kind of dressed up, is he a salesman?"

"No, he and his wife came here for years. Used to joke about them buying the place."

"What happened to the wife?"

"Passed three years ago. He still comes here few times a month."

Sarah's face drooped slightly. Kelly glanced in Mr. Costel's direction. She imagined how he must felt. He sure put on a good face of being cheerful, though.

As Michael listened to the waitress, his gaze focused on the man. The old gentleman slowly sipped his iced tea, and every now and then he touched the lady's hat. Michael was curious about him. He asked the waitress, "Think he'd join us?"

"I don't see why not. He likes meeting people. You go ahead and ask him. Be back to take your order in a bit," she replied.

Michael grabbed his glass of lemonade and headed to Mr. Costel's table. He approached the man from the front. As he neared, Mr. Costel's gaze met his. Michael nodded, and Mr. Costel did the same and said, "Well hello there, young man. What can I do for you?"

Michael gestured toward Sarah and Kelly. "Hi there, sir. My

friends and I wonder if you'd like to join us."

Costel glanced toward Kelly and Sarah. They waved and he nodded in kind, waving back. "Why that'd be fine; happy to join the party!" Mr. Costel grabbed the hat, put his laptop into a shoulder bag and stood up slowly. He groaned slightly as he stood. "Damn arthritis." He was dressed well, in a suit and tie. Michael offered to grab his shoulder bag, which Mr. Costel handed to him. "Thank you young man. What's your name?"

"Michael," Michael replied, shaking his hand.

"I'm Joseph; nice to meet you."

They walked to the table where Sarah and Kelly sat smiling. When Costel caught sight of them, he said, "Well, young man. You're sure in the company of some beautiful ladies!"

Sarah and Kelly giggled like school girls. Michael said, "Mr. Costel, allow me to introduce my friends Sarah and Kelly."

Sarah extended her hand, which Mr. Costel gingerly took into his. "Mr. Costel, nice to meet you." Mr. Costel winked and nodded politely.

Kelly also reached for Mr. Costel's hand, "Hello Mr. Costel."

Mr. Costel smiled and said, "Please, call me Joseph! I'm not a stranger around here and you calling me mister makes me feel like I'm chairman of the board or something."

They all laughed and sat back down. Michael set the shoulder bag down next to Mr. Costel before returning to his own seat.

Costel said, "I don't recognize you. Where are you from?"

Michael replied, "Louisiana, sir. Returning from a trip to New York City."

"New York City, huh? The big town. What brought you there?"

Michael glanced at Sarah and Kelly. "Kelly here had a medical emergency."

Costel's eyebrows shot up. "Oh no, you look fit as a fiddle, my dear. You alright?"

Kelly smiled. "Yes, I'm fine now."

"Well that's good. Got to take care of yourself." With that he closed his eyes, took a deep sigh and clutched the hat tighter.

The three of them looked at each other for a moment. "You okay, Joseph?" Michael asked.

Costel quickly opened his eyes, and glanced at the three of them. "Yes, sorry. I was just thinking about someone."

"Your wife?" Michael asked.

Costel looked at Michael directly in the eyes, and winced slightly. "Yes, young man. My wife. The love of my life. We were married thirty years. Always kind and giving. She really enjoyed nice clothes and hats. I remember going to church services with her, and she insisted on wearing these hats. Something about 'looking right for the Lord'. I keep one with me sometimes, when I miss her more than usual."

Kelly touched Costel's arm. "That's very sweet."

He glanced briefly at her and smiled. He continued, "We knew each other from grade school. We were friends for many years. After several times of me asking her out on a date, she finally said yes. We were going steady not long after that."

Sarah asked, "You kept after her. What made you think she was the one?"

Costel sat back for a moment. He studied the hat in his hands. It was a sort of bonnet, white in color with a cobalt blue silk flower at the front. His hands gently caressed the flower. He then looked back at Sarah. "We just had so much in common. Seemed wrong when we weren't together. She made me so happy, I just wanted to try and make her half as happy as she made me."

Sarah was struck by his words. She stole a quick glance at Michael, who looked at her as Costel spoke. He averted his eyes, and took a sip of his drink. To Sarah, at least, this started to sound more than a little familiar.

The mood at the table had gotten somber and wistful. Costel straightened up suddenly in his chair. "Well, since you're my newest friends and you're dining here at Gayle's for... the first time, is it?"

The three others nodded in agreement. Costel continued, "Your first time dining at Gayle's. Allow me to recommend the club sandwich. Out of this world." He beamed.

Michael glanced at the menu. "I see its one of their signature items."

"You betcha." Costel remarked.

"Sounds good to me!"

Sarah and Kelly chimed in, "Why not?"

Just then, the waitress returned to their table. "Keeping them company, Joseph?"

Costel winked. "My dear, we're getting along famously. And they'll all have that bang up club sandwich, Gayle's style."

The waitress jotted the order on her pad. "Sounds great. How about drink refills?"

Michael replied, I'll have another."

Kelly added, "Me too."

Sarah waved "No", taking a sip of her tea as the waitress left them.

Michael laughed at Costel's disarming nature. "Well, Joseph, I couldn't help but notice your laptop. See, I worked in electronics retail, and yours looks a little old."

Costel glanced at the bag and back at Michael. "Yeah, probably so. My daughter bought it for me secondhand, so I can keep in touch with my grandkids, her and her husband. We'll see. Never quite got the hang of computers. Was thinking of taking it to an electronics store, see if I can get some tech support."

Michael smiled. "If you'd like I can give you a few pointers."

Costel nodded. "Sounds fine, but after we eat, okay? So, you're heading back home to Metairie after this, eh?"

Sarah commented, "Yes, before my bosses decide to replace me."

Costel chuckled. "I see. Yeah that wouldn't be a good thing. You know, I used to own a chain of drug stores. Some in the south too. Not New Orleans, but around Baton Rouge. I went there several times years ago. Took a trip to New Orleans around Mardi Gras time. Some city you got there."

Michael smiled. "It has its moments, but at the end of the day there's nowhere else to be."

Sarah nodded. Kelly glanced at them, realizing New Orleans would again be her home for a time. She said, "It's nice to go back."

Costel took a sip of his drink. "Indeed. Well I'll be heading back to Robbinsville."

"Home?" Michael asked.

Costel nodded, "Got a nice little house. I try to get away when

I can, but it's getting tougher. My body ain't what it used to be," he shrugged.

Michael looked at the girls and grimaced. "Sorry to hear that."

Costel shrugged, "Eh, what can ya do? I come here several times a month. The wife and I came here a lot. It's nice. Good food, pleasant people."

The three nodded. Their food arrived soon after. They talked more with Mr. Costel as they ate. The club sandwiches were stuffed with fresh slices of turkey and generous amounts of bacon, lettuce, tomato and other toppings. The taste fluctuated from a mild salty flavor to the creamy flavor of the mayonnaise and crispy savory flavors of the bacon. The sandwiches were quite good.

Costel stopped eating to watch the others enjoying their meal. He smiled contentedly at their expressions. "So how about that food? Not too shabby, huh?"

They all nodded. Kelly raised her hand up while she chewed the bite of food in her mouth at the moment. Once she had swallowed she remarked, "So so good. And I'm a culinary student, or I was. I need to perfect one of these for whenever I get a restaurant gig."

"Told you, one of a kind! What do you mean, you were a culinary student? Did you quit?"

"Oh, no I didn't quit. The medical emergency I had got me bounced from school. I need to be cleared before I can head back. That's why I was in New York in the first place."

"Now I see. Well that's too bad. Hope it works out for you soon."

"Thank you very much, Joseph."

They enjoyed the rest of their time with Mr. Costel, and the brief pause from the worries of the road, Kelly's situation, and whatever would come for Michael's accident back at home.

Chapter Twenty-two

"DUDE! NO WAY!"

Michael listened to Jack's voice on his cell phone, and marveled at the news. They were in the Gayle's Diner parking lot after their meal with Costel. Michael sat in the backseat while Kelly and Sarah glanced back at him from the front. Michael smiled at Jack's admiration as his eyes wandered over to the moving truck, parked nearby.

"She was in your car."

"Yep."

"Your car."

"Well, Sarah's car."

"How? Why?"

"Right place, right time."

"No, can't be that simple."

"She needed a lift and happened to be Kelly's neighbor."

"Insane. Can't wait to hear it all. How's Kelly?"

"Not great. They canceled her financial aid and she's out for a semester, so she's moving back home."

"Wow, that sucks. So you guys to the rescue."

"Pretty much."

"Well things roll on over here. Ashlyn and I are... talking."

"Um, talking? That doesn't sound good."

"It's becoming a continual fight. I dunno man."

"What's wrong?"

"She doesn't like how I don't know 'where this is going' after just a few months."

"Ahh, well good luck there. Hey, you wanna talk with anyone else?"

"Put Sarah on."

Michael handed his phone to Sarah. She said, "Hello Jack."

"So... anything GOOD happen?"

"We were together. And there was a... look? What do you think?"

"Ha! I knew it! He was checking you out, but he wouldn't even admit it to ME! I think even Helen Keller would be trying to fix y'all up."

"Not now, alright? We're just outside New York City. Gonna be a few more days on the road before we're back, and I don't need this right now."

"That's fine. Look, gimme something to take my mind off things."

"Mind off what?"

"Ashlyn. Things aren't great."

Sarah eyed Michael, then glanced away and replied, "Oh honey, that's awful. Hope it gets fixed soon. You don't think talking to me is the problem, do you?"

"Well you're not her favorite, but there's more to it than that."

"Well we need to get together soon when we get back. Maybe this'll be better by then."

"Yeah, maybe. Okay, y'all get back to driving."

"See you in a few days!"

Chapter Twenty-three

About an hour after they left Gayle's, Michael's phone buzzed with a call.

"Yeah?"

"Hey."

Jack's tone told Michael right away it wasn't great news. Ashlyn troubles, maybe? His job?

"What's up?"

"I, um, heard back about the accident. Ya know, Mr. Miller?"

"Okay."

"He's suing us, man. Claiming reckless operation, endangerment, things like that."

"Reckless? Somebody hit me. I wasn't joyriding on I-10 with his ass."

Jack fumbled with papers for a bit. "You sure that's all it was, man? Shit, this is bad."

"It's fine, Jack. I'm headed home, and we'll take a look at it when I get back. How - much is he suing for?"

"80 thousand."

"And our insurance?"

"Good up to 50 only."

The number echoed in Michael's head. A horn blared as his arm jerked slightly, the truck wobbled slightly closer to the next lane on the highway. "Oh crap. It's gonna... it'll be okay, man. Let's figure something out. How much time do we have?"

"Looks like we have a few months."

Michael sighed. "Okay."

"I'll start looking up lawyers. How much money you have left?"

"Few thousand maybe. Lawyer's gonna eat that fast."

"I have a little, but yeah. Dammit."

"How's the Town Car, she fixed up?"

"Yep. Managed a few jobs over the weekend"

"We'll need to keep that up for sure with all this."

"Uh huh."

"We're a few days out still. But we'll make it through, man. I have an idea."

"Oh? What?"

"You'll see. Lemme go for now, so I don't cause any more accidents."

Jack scoffed. "You better not, gonna beat your ass."

"No way. Besides, Sarah's car had engine trouble on the way up anyway."

"GAH NOT LISTENING BAD KARMA ON YOU, BYE!" Jack yelled.

***

Jack sat at his work cubicle after his call with Michael. He was happy to see Michael hadn't lost sight of what was really important. Maybe he'd finally grown up. It seemed a no brainer to him that Michael and Sarah belonged together. He thought of the times in high school when he dated Sarah, and her and Michael chatted away about some movie or TV show, almost as if they had their very own language or something.

Too bad things hadn't gone quite as well for himself lately.

He hadn't spoken with Ashlyn in the few days since it happened. Well, a few calls went through to her voicemail.

173

Things had changed between them these past few weeks.

He went back to his email for a few minutes until his phone rang.

"Hey."

"Is that all you can say, 'hey'?"

"Well I'd left you several-"

"-Yeah, Jack. They were great. But you never even acknowledged what you did, or said you're sorry."

"Look, we had a work problem. I didn't have time to call."

"And you failed to call me until 10 that night to let me know. I made plans for us baby. With friends. Do you have any idea how that makes me look?"

Jack leaned back in his chair, and rubbed his eyes. "I'm sorry, I had to. This is my job, baby."

"Sure, fine. Your job. You made that very clear. I'm still hurt you didn't have the courtesy to let me know earlier."

Jack spun in his chair, and pondered his next response. "Is that all this is about?"

"What?"

"The silent treatment for awhile. And now, you unloading on me. Just Because I skipped out on you and your friends?"

"Oh well if you want to cut out five more minutes of your busy day, Jack, I'll tell you what else. It's not just missing drinks, Jack. It's a pattern of you regularly not being available when I want to spend time with you. It's always limos or business seminars, or drinks with your friends, one of whom you dated once."

Jack swallowed hard. She gave it to him with both barrels.

"Are we gonna get engaged or what?"

"Ashlyn. I just need a little more time-"

"Yeah, yeah, got it. You need to make your business happen and become rich. Am I supposed to just wait around for that, Jack? Meanwhile you and I get together and fuck at your convenience? Just so I know... yeah, is that it?"

"Hey!"

"Or are you waiting to see if it goes bad, so you can get back with Sarah again? Keep your options open?"

"Stop. She's a friend, Ashlyn. That's all. First, she and Michael are getting together. Second, I'm with you. Yeah, I have a fucked up schedule at times. Yeah, I sometimes need to skip out of things. I think I've been alright about letting you know. I slipped a few times. Are we gonna go through this every time I forget?"

Ashlyn's breaths became audible on the other line. Her voice shook as she said, "I want someone who wants me, Jack. Who wants to grow with me. I love you, I do. But you've got to show me. Prove to me you want this too. Lately you haven't."

Jack wriggled in his seat. "What? I haven't? Look I'm trying. I - I'll try harder, okay? Since you're talking to me again, how about we meet for coffee tonight?"

She sighed. "Yeah fine. Just remember - show me."

Chapter Twenty-four

Their caravan was a little less than two days from New Orleans. As Jack predicted, they hadn't made it home for Thanksgiving. But they were together, and would be back soon enough.

As Sarah, Kelly, and Michael made their way down the highway, Sarah called home to check on her boys. Her mom answered the phone, and muffled yelling was heard in the background. "Hello?"

Sarah smiled at the sound of her two boys. "Hi Mom, just giving you a heads up. We're about two days from home."

"Good!"

"Hope the boys haven't been too much trouble."

"Oh, they're driving me nuts, but they calm down here and there. I'm glad you're coming back soon. I'm a little old to keep this up too long. How's Kelly?"

"She's okay. We have to get a storage unit for her things and figure out where she'll stay."

"Nothing to think about, she can stay here."

Sarah beamed. While so much in their lives was tumultuous, Louise was very much the rock for both of them. "Alright, mom.

You want to talk to her? She's right here."

"Sure!"

Sarah handed the phone to Kelly. She held it up to her ear. "Hi mama!"

"Hey, my sweet baby! I'm so glad you're coming back."

"Thanks mama. Wish it was better circumstances."

"Listen, I told this to your sister. I want you to stay with me. You need to focus on getting better right now, and not some apartment lease or your bills. Until you get back on your feet, okay?"

Kelly's voice wavered. "Thanks, mama. I love you."

"Love you too, my baby. I'm going to make a huge pot of gumbo for when you two get back, alright?"

"Can't wait."

"Mmmhmm. Well drive safe, wish y'all could've been here today for Thanksgiving, but I'll see y'all soon enough!"

"Okay mama, we'll talk soon. I love you!" Kelly hung the phone up. Turning to Sarah she said, "So I'm staying with her."

"She told me. Did you think she wouldn't offer?"

"No, you're right. Guess I've been so out of my head with the hospital visit and school pulling this enrollment crap. Nice to know I can still count on some things. And people."

Kelly touched Sarah's arm. Sarah glanced briefly at her, smiled and returned her gaze to the road. "You'll be alright, sis. It's a setback. To be honest, I don't remember you having many."

"You think so?"

"Come on. You always were the star pupil in school. And you were into extracurricular activities way more than me. I was the sci-fi geek out of the limelight and languishing with the other C students. Always wanted to be more, but I ended up a single mom, working paycheck to paycheck to support me and my kids."

"You make it sound like I was a National Merit Finalist and Miss America. Believe me, I had my struggles."

"Meanwhile I'm shacking up with a meth head and making babies."

"I just had a different path. Look, I admire you for what you've been able to accomplish."

"You... do?"

177

"Of course! You were left with a rough situation. But you didn't give in and try hooking up with any guy who could support you. You survived."

"Well, yeah. But I almost stole money from a customer at Ales once."

"What?"

"Guy left his wallet. It was pretty full of bills. Had it in my hands."

"But you didn't, right?"

"No. But I thought about it for awhile."

"But you didn't. Because that's who you are. You were able to get the administrative assistant job, and work at the bar to support yourself and your boys. That took gumption, Sarah. Don't ever discount who you are, alright?"

Sarah smiled. The power of Kelly's words really took hold of her. Her voice quavered as she said, "Well thank you. That... that means a lot."

Chapter Twenty-five

They arrived back in Metairie early on a Saturday afternoon. They were slightly dazed from the long trip. They arranged a storage unit for Kelly, drove the U-Haul over and unloaded it. Then they dropped the U-Haul truck off, and Michael brought Sarah and Kelly to her apartment before he returned to his.

John had left Michael a voicemail about being back at Ochsner. Michael hadn't heard anything during the trip, so he figured things were about the same, or maybe his dad tried to save the worst news for when he wasn't on the road.

He made his way into his mom's hospital room, and caught his dad's gaze. John sat bedside, Barbara's hand in his. "Come on in," he said softly with a smile.

Michael took a seat next to his dad. Barbara was awake, but moved rather slow. John gently brushed hair on her head as he held her hand.

"How's she doing?"

"Better. Little by little."

"You never called while I was gone."

John glanced at Michael. "Didn't want to worry you. She fell back into a coma for a few days, but it looks like she's coming out now."

Michael sighed. "Dad I'm-"

"Son, it's okay. You did what you had to do. Your mom's still here."

"Do they even know if she's gonna shake this?"

John returned to her hair. "They're not giving up. I won't let them."

Her eyes, somewhat glazed, cleared for a moment as if she'd tuned into their conversation. She whispered, "Michael?"

"I'm here mom," Michael said, touching the blanket covering her legs.

"Glad you... are here."

"Me too, mom. Glad you're here."

"He's been away helping a friend, dear." John remarked. "Saving the day."

She managed a faint smile. "That's my baby."

Michael felt good about the gleam of recognition of him in his mom. She was still in there, like his dad said.

John kissed her forehead. "I'm gonna catch up with Michael, alright dear? Be right here if you need me."

Barbara nodded.

They sat back in their chairs as Barbara watched them. John asked, "How did your trip go?"

"Well, Kelly had to leave school. Sarah and I helped her move back here."

"Wow, so she's back here for good?"

"For now anyway. I think she'll be able to enroll there again soon. They just didn't want to hold her spot while her condition was still uncertain."

"Why uncertain?"

"Seizures, she started having them."

"Oh no."

"Yeah, she needs to rest up a bit."

"How about your work situation?"

Michael sighed, "They let me go."

John replied, "I thought they might. Still, I must say I'm proud of how you stuck your neck out for your friends like that."

"Things just got away from me, dad. Jack and I got into some trouble with the limo business, and now I'm out of this job-"

"Trouble? What kind?"

"An accident. Some guy threatening us, a lawsuit."

John's jaw tightened. He checked Barbara for a moment, then leaned closer to him. "Are you alright?"

Michael shrugged. "I'm not sure, dad. Jack's working on things."

John nodded. "I know an attorney. Want his number?"

"Um sure, whenever you can, dad."

John gazed back to Barbara. "Meeting with her doctors in a few days to see what's next."

"Dad I'm gonna come by here more. Sit with her. You need a break now and then, how much are you here now?"

"Most evenings, and a lot on weekends."

"I'm gonna chip in, dad. I owe you that. And her."

John smiled. "You got a deal. But what about getting another job?"

"Oh, I have a plan. Don't worry."

***

Michael called Jack's cell phone. The phone rang a few times before Jack answered. "Hey, man. You back in town?"

"I am, dude. Are you at your place? Can I drop by?"

"Well, Ashlyn's over right now." Michael heard Jack's muffled voice as he spoke with someone on his end. After a few moments he told Michael, "Come on over!"

Michael hung up, and proceeded to Jack's apartment. He and Jack embraced, and Michael walked into the apartment. Ashlyn sat at one of the kitchen table chairs. When she and Michael caught sight of each other she rose and walked toward him. "How was New York?"

"It was unexpected," Michael laughed. "Got to chauffeur a celeb."

"So I heard."

Jack headed to his refrigerator as Michael and Ashlyn talked. He handed Michael a bottle of Abita Turbodog brown ale, and motioned Michael to the sofa. Once Michael sat down, Jack sat beside him, and Ashlyn moved to an easy chair adjacent to the sofa.

Michael glanced at both of them. "Thanks for the beer, and for letting me stop by unannounced."

"It's alright, man," Jack replied. "I missed hanging with you."

"Good to be back home, man. Wanted to tell y'all some stuff."

Jack said, "Sure, man. What's up?"

Michael said, "I know I've done some 'not smart' things. Skipping out on a job, pissing and moaning over my station in life instead of getting off my ass more, and doing something about it. Well, that's gonna change."

Jack replied, "You sound like me with these aspirations. You got nothing to lose by trying, dude." They both laughed.

Michael said, "We've got the limo business and that's great, even with this incident hanging over us."

"I talked with a lawyer, so we have someone on our side."

Michael nodded. "Great."

Jack glanced at Ashlyn a moment. "And you and Sarah?"

Michael smirked. "Well, we hooked up."

Ashlyn cocked her head as Jack nudged Michael. "Hey there ya go. So what now?"

"We'll see. Think she wanted to just get back, and deal with Kelly's move first."

Jack looked at Ashlyn. She managed a smile and said, "Good for you."

"Yeah, well... there's something you should know, man."

"Um yeah? Like what?" Michael asked as he sank a little more into the couch.

"I saw Louise a few days ago, before you called. Jimmy got released while you were gone. He called looking for Sarah and the boys."

Michael froze. "Thought he had a few more months to go."

"Not so much."

Michael patted his thighs in thought. "She can't want anything to do with him. No, it's been long enough. Enough's happened. Right?"

Jack shrugged. "I agree. Just watch it, okay?"

"I don't want to lose her a second time."

"Get it done, man!" Jack smiled.

"Do it," Ashlyn said. "Close the deal," she added, eying Jack.

"Okay, alright. Damn, I thought I was the more aggressive one now."

Jack laughed. "I missed giving you shit in person."

Michael laughed and asked Ashlyn, "And you put up with this guy?" She rolled her eyes.

Jack continued, "Alright, enough. Close the deal with Sarah."

"Yeah, I know. But she can be moody. Don't want to scare her with something big like this."

"Blah blah just do it already!" Jack exhorted.

"How?"

Ashlyn said, "Just tell her, Michael."

"Tell her what though?"

"Women want to know they're wanted. Desired. You already have the physical with her, get the emotional now. Let her know how you really feel."

Jack said, "So how're you gonna do it?"

Michael thought a moment. "Guess I just lay out my cards on the table. Maybe I crash and burn, and look like an idiot. But if I don't try, and she ends up with someone else, I'll hate myself for not going for it."

"Make it happen!"

Jack and Michael shook hands warmly. Ashlyn smiled at Michael, while she reserved a more scornful look for Jack.

Chapter Twenty-six

Sarah and Kelly stayed at her apartment while Sarah checked on things she left before the trip. Sarah picked up her mail from the apartment office and cleared messages from her machine. Mostly it was solicitors and one credit card representative. Of course, late payments again.

Kelly sat at a chair by the kitchen table. Sarah glanced around, saying, "Bathroom and then off to mom's to see my kiddos."

A knock on the door startled them. They looked at each other in puzzlement. Sarah stood with her hands on her hips and faced the door as if she had x-ray vision. "Who the hell would be coming by on a Tuesday night?"

Kelly shrugged. "Maybe its Michael, and one of us left something in his car."

Sarah walked to the door and opened it to see Peter. He looked slightly bewildered, as if he looked for the right apartment and maybe tried a few wrong ones first.

Sarah gaped for a moment, then regained her composure. "What're you doing here?"

Peter smiled. "Just wanted to come by, figured you'd be back soon. Can I come in?"

"It's not a great time right now, Peter. My sister and I are about to go over to my mom's. Can I call you later or something?"

Peter glanced into her apartment for a second and then back at her. He nodded to the side and said, "I really need to ask you something. Just a few minutes, huh?"

Sarah became more puzzled. Peter at her apartment in the first place was cause for surprise. He seemed nervous, and not his usual cocky arrogant self. Sarah leaned back into the doorway, glanced at Kelly and said, "I'll be out here for a sec." Kelly nodded and tried to hide her smirk.

Sarah closed the door and faced Peter. "What's going on?"

Peter folded his arms. He looked down in thought. He took a deep breath and glanced up at Sarah. "Look, I missed having you around the past several days. I guess you being out made me think about things."

Sarah folded her arms. "Okayyyy. What kind of things?"

Peter glanced toward both ends of the hall. "We should do this at work."

"No, you're here. What's on your mind?"

"I wanna take you out sometime."

Sarah swallowed hard. "Yeah first thing, never me ask that at work. Damn, ever hear of sexual harassment?" Now she was the one who glanced around.

"Come on," Peter pleaded. "I'm serious."

"You came here to ask me this?"

"Yeah. You want to get a drink or dinner, maybe this weekend?"

Sarah was stunned. Peter asked her out. Her mind thought back to all those times he gave her a hard time at work. She remembered those times he hovered around her desk, or when he bragged about his latest wild night out. Was it all a plan of his to have impressed her? And now, as she and Michael grew closer, Peter laid this on her. Her mind raced, and tried to even sort out the numerous considerations that ran through it, not to mention what her plans for any of these ideas were. She thought, *am I, a single mom several years running, really ready to jump back into dating, and with one of these two men?*

She paused, and leaned on the wall with one hand. She gazed off to the side in thought. A slight smirk crept onto her face, and her tongue stuck out slightly between her teeth as she contemplated her response to Peter's surprising request.

She said, "Peter. I'm... flattered. I am. It's just - I don't think this is the best time for me."

Peter nodded. He shoved his hand in to his pocket, and rattled his keys a bit. "Oh okay. Well ya know, never mind. I'll see you back at work. Tomorrow?"

"I'll be there." Sarah's brow furrowed as she watched Peter, a little uneasy on his feet, he rattled his keys a little more.

"Yeah." He turned and walked down the hallway to exit the building.

Sarah looked at him as he walked away. *Well that was unexpected,* she thought. On one hand, it was nice to know that she'd attracted several guys' attention. But her boss? This was fairly odd to consider. Sure was a far cry off from her Dave Grohl fantasy.

***

Sarah and Kelly left the apartment for Louise's house. Sarah filled Kelly in on Peter's surprising proposition.

Kelly giggled, "Now your boss wants to hook up with you? My baby sister, sleeping her way to the top!"

"Oh piss off, bitch! Not going there, with him and his Zach Galifianakis looking ass!"

"Sarah, you're a hot little number. About time you realize it."

"I'm gonna slap you."

"Two guys after you. And 'father of the year' makes three!"

"Bleach your tongue for even mentioning him."

"Jimmy's a useless ass. But what about Peter?

"Never thought about him once."

"He's employed, and pretty well I bet. Sales manager?"

"I've been doing alright on my own."

"Yeah, but you're lonely sis. I can see it."

"Thing is, Michael and I have a lot of history. Do I risk losing that on a relationship that might crash and burn? And Peter is my

186

boss. Yeah, I miss being with someone, but do I take the chance and maybe lose my job?"

"You'd lose your job?"

"Can't imagine the radio station would be thrilled about an employee dating her supervisor."

"I'm not hearing you say you don't want to consider it."

"Okay... let me be more clear. No. Too much drama and risk." Sarah sighed, "I need Vanessa's take."

"Who?"

"Promotions girl at the station. Knows Peter well. I get the feeling she's gonna jump on me with this tomorrow."

"I see. So that's Peter. What about you and Michael?"

"Yeah, that's a whole other side of things. We have a great bond going."

"I bet you do," Kelly giggled.

"Shut it. Yeah, I got horny. It'd been a while. You know my history."

"He's cute and sweet. He ditched a job to help you and me."

"Yeah, but I'm trying to take things slow and be careful about who I get with."

"Well, baby sis, I think fate or whatever is throwing these guys at you and it has to be for good reason."

"Then fate can just hold up a damn minute. Kelly, when did I become the girl men fight over?"

They arrived at Louise's house. As they opened the front door, they heard Alex and Taylor's frantic voices as the two boys ran in their direction. When they caught sight of Sarah, they yelled, "Mommy!!!"

Sarah choked up slightly as she stooped down, and held her arms out to catch them both in an embrace. The boys ran at her with enough force, and knocked her back slightly into Kelly. Sarah laughed, "Oh my goodness. My two little men, I missed you so much!" She kissed them both. Sarah laughed, "Careful now, don't wanna hurt Aunt Kelly any more than she already is!"

The boys glanced up at Kelly. She smiled down at the happy reunion and said, "Hi there!"

"Hi Aunt Kelly," Taylor and Alex responded in unison.

Sarah stood back up. Taylor and Alex both hugged Kelly.

Alex asked her, "Aunt Kelly, we heard you had a scissor."

Kelly and Sarah shared a smile. Kelly patted Alex's arm. "Yes baby, I had a seizure. I was sick, but I'm gonna be better now. I'll be staying here awhile so we can visit more, okay?"

Alex nodded and smiled.

Sarah said, "Maybe if you two are good Aunt Kelly can take you to City Park to feed the ducks." The boys smiled at the idea.

Louise was in the kitchen. She sprinkled some filé on the gumbo when she saw them in the den. "Well hello weary travelers!" She hugged Kelly and Sarah. "Glad y'all are here. How was the road trip?"

"Long, and talkative," Kelly chuckled. "Glad I'm back, in spite of why."

Louise winced, and brushed Kelly's arm. "I know, baby. I've been praying and worrying for you. We need to get your strength back."

Kelly eyed the pot. "Gumbo is a great start." She grinned.

"I'm proud of my girls pulling together when times are rough." She smiled at Sarah.

Taylor and Alex had resumed playing with some toys near the TV. Sarah glanced at them. "So they didn't run you too ragged?"

"They've been quite the handful. We had movies and went to Chuck E Cheese for pizza and video games. Their homework is winding down for the holiday break. They wore me out." She laughed weakly. "It was fun, but I'm so glad you're back."

As Sarah eyed her boys, Louise said, "Listen, need to tell you about Jimmy."

The name jolted her out of her happy reunion. She shot a glance toward Louise. "What about him?"

Louise sighed after a peek in the boys' direction. "He called over here."

"Oh really?"

"Mmhmm. Didn't tell me he was out."

"I'm not exactly his parole officer, mom," Sarah fidgeted with her hands a bit. Taylor smiled at her, and she did her best to return it. She hoped he wouldn't see on her face the concern she now felt. "What did he want?"

"What do you think?"

"Never gonna happen," Sarah muttered, and shook her head.

Louise stroked her shoulder. "Hon, will you listen to me finally, and get a restraining order on him?"

Sarah bit her lip, her eyes closed. "Yeah. Okay. Whatever it takes."

Louise touched Sarah's chin. "Baby, I didn't want to bring this up, but you needed to hear it as soon as possible."

"It's fine. Thanks, mom," she smiled.

Louise glanced at the kids and said, "Gumbo's ready. Everyone ready to eat?"

The boys glanced at her and nodded. Kelly and Sarah followed Louise into the kitchen to help set the table. Sarah glanced at Taylor and Alex, who watched them. "Hey, you two. I didn't see you go wash your hands. Come on, be good and clean up now before dinner."

Taylor and Alex ran to the bathroom, as they playfully shoved each other along the way. Louise scooped rice into bowls. "So, Sarah, everything alright with work?"

Kelly chuckled slightly with thoughts of Sarah's recent development with Peter. Sarah glared at Kelly and replied, "I think so. Ales doesn't have me back on schedule until this Friday, and I'm supposed to head back into WZEB tomorrow."

"How's that boss of yours at WZEB, Peter, was it? He still giving you a hard time?"

Kelly shrugged at Sarah. Sarah thought, why not clue mom in. Maybe she can offer advice. "Pretty much. You know, he did something strange just a little while ago. He stopped by my apartment to ask me out."

Louise stopped with the bowls and looked at Sarah. "Oh really?"

"Yeah, I know. Bizarre for someone who gave me so much trouble to now want a date."

"Must just be how he flirts." Louise remarked.

"I feel strange about it, I mean I never thought of him like that, and now I'll be working for a guy who did that to me."

"Is he cute?"

Sarah chuckled. "Oh, um, not very. But he can be funny. I've seen him at radio station functions; he is usually the guy who has

189

people laughing in the room."

"Are you interested?"

"Not really but I also don't want him to cause problems if I say no."

"Just be careful." Louise carried the pot back to the stove, adding, "Of course, you're single, and life is short."

Sarah nodded. *True, life is short,* she thought. But she had already experienced a good amount of "life is short" rationalizations that lead her to her current situation. She needed a stable relationship and steady father figure for her boys, and had she wasn't solid that Peter fit the bill.

Louise brought the gumbo to the table, set glasses of water out for the boys and wine for herself, and soft drinks for Kelly and Sarah. Kelly served salad onto the plates, and Sarah sliced some pieces of French bread for them. Taylor and Alex sat at the table. After grace, they dug in. Sarah kept an eye on Taylor and Alex as she sat between them.

Louise took a sip of wine. "So, Kelly, everything alright with the storage unit?"

"Yeah, mom. Michael, Sarah, and one of the employees there lent a hand getting it all in."

"Good. Sorry I couldn't come out to help, just been trying to fix the food and keep an eye on those two." Louise motioned to Taylor and Alex.

"You did plenty. And the gumbo is delicious!"

Sarah nodded and agreed with Kelly's assessment of the food. Taylor and Alex slowly ate spoonfuls while they glanced at each other from around Sarah.

Louise smiled at Kelly. "Thank you, baby. Bet those culinary school people would learn a thing or two from Cajun chefs down in Louisiana, and especially New Orleans. I still can't believe they're making you sit out a semester."

"Well, it's just the medical clearance issue. I hate it too, but looks like I don't have a choice."

"Well I think they're running that school like a short order diner if you ask me. They better get their act together, as much as you've had to do to get into that place."

Kelly nodded. She did have to apply several times to the

culinary institute for acceptance, and then there was an interview process that took a month or two. "I'm closer to finishing than I am to the start. It's just another hurdle, mom."

Louise took a piece of French bread, and chewed it thoughtfully. "Right. Well the guest bedroom is pretty much set up."

"Great!" Kelly smiled.

"Taylor and Alex even helped. Told them it was for their Aunt Kelly."

Sarah and Kelly looked at the boys. Kelly said, "Aww wasn't that nice? I think I need to treat them to something for that." She asked them, "How does hot chocolate and going to a Christmas village sound?"

The boys' eyes widened. Taylor asked, "Ooh, tonight?"

Sarah shrugged. "Not tonight. It's been a long few days, and I need to take care of a few things at my place. How about we do it very soon?"

"Aw mom, can't we go tonight?" Alex pleaded.

"No, and that's it. Let's enjoy tonight, and you can tell me about school since I've been away. I know you have some class projects due before the holidays."

Louise nodded and smiled at Sarah.

***

Sarah strolled through the front door of WZEB-FM Monday morning after her return from New York. She wondered about her return. She'd been out for a week before. Maybe there was some new report for corporate now, or another bang up sales proposal from Peter?

Of course, this time there was also Peter's other proposal for after hours.

She greeted the receptionist, and headed straight to her desk. It was ten minutes past eight. The salespeople were in their morning meeting, which gave her a few minutes before the regular onslaught of sales package requests and account claims hit.

She went to the lunch room and coffee pot for her fuel. As she poured a cup, she heard Vanessa, the promotions director. "Hey, girl! Welcome back."

Sarah smiled. "Thanks!"

"How was your trip?"

Sarah turned and smiled, "It was an adventure. Me and a friend helped my big sis move back home."

"Oh, I thought it was a vacation. Hope it went alright."

"Yeah, pretty much. I miss anything around here?"

"Hmm. Well Peter was missing you, I can tell you.

Sarah sipped her coffee. "Oh?"

"Yeah. We had a live broadcast at that new Toyota Dealership on Veterans Boulevard. He came out to check on the client and hung around a little while. Said you put the sales package together for that one."

"Really? I guess he liked it."

"Yeah. Well, I think it's more than just your office work."

"Oh?"

Vanessa glanced around the lunch room. One of the radio station engineers looked over some paperwork at a nearby table. "Come by my office? Before you get pounced on by salespeople?"

Sarah regarded Vanessa with curiosity. It seemed she had a bit of gossip that was for Sarah's ears only. "Okay, quick. I have a feeling I'm going to get an extra load, being my first day back."

They slipped into Vanessa's office. It was a cozy room, with enough concert and movie posters on the walls it was considered wall paper, by Vanessa at least. Strewn about the room were various boxes of promotional giveaway items. Vanessa cleared a box of radio station koozies off a chair in her office for Sarah. *Wow, this place reminds me of my apartment. I really need to straighten that place up, like tonight,* Sarah mused.

Vanessa sat at the chair by her desk. She heard an email notification sound from her computer. "Ahh, more contest entries. They can wait." She turned back to Sarah.

Sarah sipped her coffee. "So what's the big secret?"

Vanessa leaned forward. "Well, Sarah, Peter called me last night. It was kind of a weird thing. I mean, he's called me after hours before. Usually it's for something about an upcoming live broadcast, or he just wants to catch a drink. But this time he tells me he stopped by your place yesterday, and he asked you out."

Sarah had taken a sip of coffee, and hoped she wouldn't spit it out at this news. Peter called Vanessa about her?

"You're kidding. He told you this?"

"Yes, he did."

"Well did he tell you what I said?"

"Not really, but I got the idea it didn't go how he wanted."

"Well, he threw that shit up out of left field. I'm sorry, for one thing, eww. I mean, he's good for laughs, but I don't see me and him together."

Vanessa nodded. "And that's up to you. I know he does off the wall things, I mean one time he proposed to this stripper."

Sarah laughed, "Oh what now? You've got to tell me THAT story."

"Lunch sometime," Vanessa giggled. "But seriously, whatever you decide to do, just know... I've worked with him for several years. He's not a bad guy. He's rough around the edges, but once you get to know him, he's decent."

"Oh, you mean when he's not drunk off his ass?"

Vanessa squinted and replied, "That would be the rough part."

Sarah finished her coffee. "Maybe I should just date for now. There's another guy I'm friends with, and I'm wondering if there's more going on there."

"Oh? Do tell."

"His name's Michael. I guess I haven't told you about him. He's been around for awhile. Like, since high school. He's the one who went with me to New York. We had lots of time for talk and stuff."

"Stuff?" Vanessa nudged Sarah.

Sarah tried to keep the smile off her face and failed. "Yeah, well we had sex."

"Well alright then, this more than just casual?"

"Yep. I'm really beginning to wonder about him and me."

"Well, maybe you can just date for a little bit to see if there's more with him. I mean, you made it this far, right?"

"Yeah I guess."

"Perhaps it's better to just ease into another relationship than dive in. Hell, I'm a classic example. Married at 21, divorced not even a year and a half later. And I didn't have kids to worry

193

about."

"That may just be the way for me." Sarah sighed. She glanced at the clock on Vanessa's desk. It was 8:25am. "Better get to my desk. Five more minutes to prepare for the sales hurricane. Thanks for the chat."

"Anytime, Sarah. Let me know how it goes with Peter!"

***

After she passed by the coffee pot again for a refill, Sarah returned to her desk. She noticed her voicemail light on. Most of her messages were the sales team group messages that Peter or the General Station Manager sent out to all the reps. There was, however, a personal one from Peter:

"Hey, Sarah. I just left your apartment. I know that probably was a lot, asking you out and all. Just... let's talk, okay? Come see me on Monday."

Sarah gazed blankly at the phone. Type A personality indeed. She needed a response.

She cleared her phone inbox but saved Peter's message. While his persistent overtures were a little off putting to her, she had an odd curiosity about the whole situation that made her wait until they spoke in person before she dismissed the idea of them altogether.

As she hung up her phone, she heard a familiar voice from just outside her cubicle. "Well look who's back." She saw Ted, with that smile that was about fifty shades of sleazy. "How was your trip? Get laid?"

Sarah scoffed. "What do you want?"

"Hey, I'm just talking, no need to get bitchy. I do have a live broadcast package for you to work up for tomorrow." He waved a stack of paper at her. "It's all written up, just needs your touch."

Sarah nodded and smirked. "Bring it here, can't promise it'll be ready before tomorrow morning, but I'll do my best."

Ted nodded. "Nice to see you back, kiddo." He walked back to his desk. Sarah checked her email for a few minutes, until she became aware of someone outside her cube. "Just leave the rough copy in my basket, I'll get it later."

"Hey," Peter quipped.

Sarah jumped slightly and saw Peter with a cup of coffee and a smile. "Oh damn, Peter. Warn me before you do that!"

Peter chuckled. "I like my people on their toes. Welcome back. I know you're getting caught up. Come see me in a few minutes."

"Okay, sure, Peter."

After several minutes with the incoming account claims and proposal rough drafts, as well as the "Welcome back, how was the trip?" conversations with the salespeople, Sarah locked her computer and stood up. She glanced at the picture of Taylor and Alex near her desk phone before she headed into Peter's office.

Peter was at his desk, on the phone. Two of the walls of his corner office consisted of windows from ceiling to floor. The blinds were open partly, which let the morning sun in a bit. Peter glanced to the windows at his right when Sarah entered and closed the door behind her. He caught a glimpse of her, and motioned to one of two chairs at the front of his desk. She walked over to the chair and sat down.

Peter mimed a "Just another minute," signal to her as he listened. He then continued on the phone, "Well Ken, you own a new daiquiris shop. I don't care how good your Cajun Eggnog Daiquiris are, all the other guys have 'em too. Without more live broadcasts bringing people in you're not going to be in business long after New Years! What do you think cutting back ads is gonna accomplish?"

Sarah sat back in the chair, and smirked at Peter. *Sounds like I'm not the only one giving him the cold shoulder at present,* she mused.

Peter paused for another moment then continued, "Alright, Ken. Lemme see what I can work up for you. You're not understanding me, I think. I'll show you some options for increasing your business." He gestured to Sarah as he spoke, and she knew what that meant.

"Ken, I'll be by tomorrow, show you what we got. Alright, see you then. Bye." Peter hung the phone up and sighed. "Damn, what does it take with some people? I'm gonna get with you on working up a proposal for this guy. It'll be similar to some bar promotions we've done in the past, so you may have something already saved you can edit without doing a lot of extra work."

Sarah nodded. "Mmhmmm. I guess that isn't why you wanted to see me though."

Peter glanced downward before peeking up at her. "Uh, no it isn't. I want to talk about what I said last night and some ideas I have. Just hear me out first, alright?"

Sarah grasped the arms of the chair, and took a slow breath.

Peter folded his hands, and leaned forward slightly. His elbows were on the desk. "I'm hard on you a lot here. I know that. I can be an asshole a lot of the time. But I'm like that with everyone pretty much, and I'm testing people to see what they can handle, see how much they can take, see how good they can be in their jobs. I mean, I'm a sales manager. If my sales people aren't good at what they do, what good am I?"

Sarah nodded slightly, her arms folded. *Where's he going with this? He's making this feel like a job interview.*

He continued. "You hit the ground running here, and I like that. I've given you a lot of work to do because you do good work. And through that, I got to know you a little bit.

Sarah shifted in her seat.

Peter continued, "Seeing you after hours at a live broadcast or when I asked you to help Vanessa set up prize giveaways at a client's store, and I stopped by."

Sarah nodded.

"I think you're a tough person, Sarah. A single mom who can balance working two jobs with taking care of two young boys. I don't know what help you have, but that's impressive."

Sarah was stunned. Peter had never expressed this kind of admiration for her. He had complimented her on a piece of work here and there in the past, but this was something new.

Sarah smiled, "Well mom helps out here and there, but yeah... I guess I manage pretty okay."

Peter nodded. "You do. And you have a strong personality. You don't let these salespeople tell you what's going on, you keep a handle on things. I like being around people who are tough. I think we might have a good time if we gave it a try."

Sarah sighed. She glanced past Peter out of the window behind him. The morning sun lit the sky up brilliantly, and the scarce clouds in the distance were barely noticeable against the blue sky. A few birds flew back and forth past the building as she scanned the scenery.

She turned to Peter. "I'm flattered you think so much of me. And I wish you could have mentioned something like this sooner. I know you like my work, but I get the feeling a lot of the time you just wanted to be an ass to me, just because you could."

"I can't be everyone's friend here if I'm supposed to push them."

"Yeah, I guess. But sometimes you push a little too hard."

"Well, I apologize. Maybe if you took the chance to get to know me better you might see another side."

Sarah thought back to Vanessa's words about Peter. Maybe there was more to him. She figured she'd have to take a chance at some point in her life.

***

She'd practiced her speech to him whenever they spoke again. She had a great place or places picked out, and when it happened maybe she'd have a glass or two of wine in her, so her temper was even more fired up when let him have it.

Of course, she never thought it would have happened while she was with her kids in the car.

Her phone rang as she worked her way back home with the boys. Hoping it was Michael, she answered, "Yeah?"

"Hey boo."

Jimmy. She took a moment to regroup. His voice pummeled her in the gut. Her heartache on the other line. She glanced at her boys in the mirror. They chatted and were oblivious, of course.

She took a deep breath.

"Hey."

"How are you?"

"I'm fine. Heard you're out."

"Parole. Got released three days ago."

"Well bully for you." The tear itched her cheek as it wormed down her face.

"Hey, I'm sorry."

197

"Oh," Sarah's voice hitched as she turned a corner in her car. "Sorry, are you? Well I'm glad you could get that off your chest."

"Baby-"

"-Don't baby me. What do you want?"

"You still have my paintings?"

"Yeah, well Goodwill didn't want them, guess they figured they were trash."

"Damn."

"Oh, did that hurt? Good."

Long pause on the other end as Sarah pulled up to a red light. Finally Jimmy said, "I wanna make this up to you."

"Oh, now you do? A little late, huh? Shouldn't you be under some kinda house arrest or something?"

"Naah, I'm with my uncle. Staying here and working. Long as I stay clean, you know... pass a piss test every week, and keep a job, I'm fine."

"Someone let you work for them? Willingly?"

"It's manual labor, but it's a check. Working on a road crew in Metairie."

Jimmy's talk about work seemed a bit surreal. Sarah pondered.

"I'm still beyond pissed."

"I know."

Sarah paused.

"Whatcha thinking?" Jimmy asked.

"Stay away from me, Jimmy. Just stay away." She hung up.

Chapter Twenty-seven

Michael scanned the road as he drove to Sarah's apartment. He felt good, better than he had in a long time. It just seemed so clear to him. The idea he had, the deal he made with Kelly, and Sarah. Even being with her kids, watching out for them, wasn't so scary anymore.

He parked on the street and made his way to her apartment. *Why bother announcing to her I'm coming?* He thought. *She's always talking about me never just going for something, well look out Sarah, there's a new Michael in town.*

Opening the door to the main hallway, he strode inside. A few residents were about, some did their laundry, and others just meandered. Michael breezed past them. *Things have to turn around here at some point. It's some kind of karma, right? I mean the universe has to dump on everyone a little, and I've got to be at my quota at some point.*

He ran up the flight of stairs. *Mom is gonna pull through. She has to. Dad didn't seem to be too sure, well I am. She's being taken care of. And she'll remember Sarah. It's been awhile, but they know about her, mom and dad.*

He arrived at her door, and heard muffled shouting from within. Had he arrived while she disciplined her boys? *Well she could always have used a hand,* he thought. He knocked on the door. No response.

A few more knocks and the door flew open, and Michael was face to face with Jimmy.

"The fuck you want?" He sneered.

Michael caught a glimpse of Sarah at the back of the room, behind a sofa. Her eyes gave Michael a thousand messages... *why are you here? I don't care, you are... help me... don't leave me alone with him.*

"What the hell are you doing here?" Michael replied to Jimmy.

"Seeing my kids, like I got a right to."

"And I'm seeing Sarah, like I got a right to."

As Michael advanced, Jimmy's hand stopped him. Michael said, "Let me in."

"Jimmy, you don't pay any bills here, so shut the fuck up." Sarah said.

Jimmy glanced at her, his sneer faded to a smirk. "Where are my boys?"

"Not here, jackass. Why don't you take off?"

Michael walked over by her kitchen table. Jimmy slammed the door, and checked around the room. "I'll leave when I'm good and ready. They're here, you just sent them out. Your bitch sister take 'em or something?"

"None of your business," Sarah replied. "I don't trust you with them. Imagine that."

Michael looked around the apartment. The floor was a mess. He guessed they had been at this for a few minutes. Sarah looked okay for the most part, but her eyes had a slight wild look in them that just about matched her hair at the moment.

Jimmy announced, "I'm their daddy, and I want to see my boys."

"Don't even start that. You've never been a daddy to them anyway."

Jimmy moved about the room, eyes fixed on Sarah. She too slid around, almost as if they were two animals in the wild that sized each other up for the kill.

Michael gazed around the kitchen. Looks like she was packing or something. He thought about her annual spring cleaning she mentioned. Boxes around his feet by the table. Boxes of vases and bottles.

"You can't stop me from seeing them."

"Oh you best think again. Think I don't know about restraining orders? I could get your ass thrown back in jail just for harassing me now."

"Hey, y'all don't want to do this," Michael said. "Jimmy, the kids obviously aren't here now-"

Jimmy's eyes never left Sarah. "Shut up, Michael. This don't concern you."

"Look, you're not gonna see them tonight. We just got back from out of town."

That got Jimmy's attention.

"We? You two went on a trip?" He glared at Michael.

Sarah remarked, "New York. My 'bitch sister' got sick and needed to move home, and Michael was man enough to help."

Michael nodded. Jimmy's scowl returned. "You... and she?"

"None of your damn business, Jimmy."

Jimmy clenched his fists. "Oh I think it is."

Michael braced himself. Jimmy was near Sarah, but he felt like Jimmy might have went for him at any moment too. He wasn't sure he could grab something quick enough if necessary.

"We're gonna settle this, sissy boy, understand?" Jimmy pointed a finger at Michael. Michael clenched his jaw and felt his hatred for Jimmy welling up. He hated him even more for what he had done to Sarah. He knew then that it wouldn't stop. Wouldn't ever stop unless someone did something.

Michael's fist had tightened around some object he'd grabbed off the counter. It felt cold and was firm. Jimmy looked at Michael, then back at Sarah. "How about we go looking for the boys now. Figure they're with Kelly, so let's just go see. You and me, Sarah." He reached for her arm.

Sarah moved away from his grasp and reached for her cell phone. "No I'm not going anywhere, and you had better leave 'cause I'm calling 911-"

Jimmy swatted the phone out of her hand, and slapped her. She yelped and fell over a small table, sending its contents sprawling onto the floor.

With one fluid motion, Michael flung his arm up. Before either of them knew what had happened, a porcelain vase flew straight at Jimmy, smashed him in the head and knocked him unconscious.

***

It took the JPSO deputy almost an hour before the incident report was finished with Sarah and Michael, and Jimmy was escorted via handcuffs from her apartment. He was headed back to jail for a bit more time, a lot of time if Sarah had any say about it.

Michael and Sarah sat on her couch as they surveyed the scene in her apartment.

"You really should be careful who you invite over these days," he joked.

"Oh, like I planned all this?" Sarah replied as she held a plastic ice bag where Jimmy hit her.

"How's the head?"

"Sore, but I'll live. Just glad the boys didn't see all that."

"They're staying with your mom?"

"Yeah, called her while the cop was taking Jimmy outside." Michael nodded.

Sarah looked at him. "So what exactly were you coming here for, besides saving my ass at the last minute?"

Michael almost answered her, but he stopped when he saw it in her eyes again.

The longing.

Emptiness that she covered up through the years showed itself to Michael. Sarah had fooled most people that it didn't exist. But the crack in that window shade was left for Michael as always. His feelings for her burst at the seams.

"Sarah, I've been a fool. An idiot. Chasing something - someone who really doesn't exist."

"Head in the clouds, maybe?" She chuckled.

"Yeah, well. I'm done with that. I know what I need now."

She faced him more, and adjusted the ice bag. "Oh do you now?" A slight smile found her face.

He took her hand and smiled. "Well, how about it? We

already know we click physically."

She studied their hands, now intertwined. "You don't know the half of it."

"What?"

She sat up, and collected herself. She smiled and gazed at the clock on the far wall.

Michael sat up with her. "What?"

She took a deep breath, blinked her eyes slowly, and began, "Michael, I think Alex may be your son."

Silence in the room at that. The only sound was the second hand of the wall clock. Michael swallowed hard and fought for words.

She continued, "Our little one night stand? Yeah. I felt something afterward. And well, Jimmy and I had been together during that time, but I don't know. And Alex has this birthmark on his arm. Same place you do. And, well, I know that doesn't really mean much. But, well. I have a feeling he's yours."

Her eyes found his again. The shades were pulled back more, and tears formed. The ice bag slid from her hand and her lip trembled. "I don't expect anything from you, Michael. I'm a big girl, and I've been - well - making my bed for awhile now. You don't have to do something you don't want."

Michael watched her, he wanted her in his arms.

Sarah wept as she whispered, "I'm sorry, I don't really know for sure-"

He grabbed her hands. "Shh. It's okay. Wow. That's- look, I want you. And this. Your kids too. And knowing that Alex might be..."

"It's a lot to ask someone, Michael."

"No, I get that. And I'm still here." He smiled.

"You're not mad I didn't tell you sooner?"

"It was a crazy time, and I don't know how well I would've dealt then anyway."

She smiled, "You were kind of a mess then."

He wiped her tears. "Hey, watch it now. So where do we go from here?"

She sniffled and said, "For now, I'd settle for being held. Tomorrow, we get my kids... and find out about you and Alex."

<u>Chapter Twenty-eight</u>

Michael sat at a desk, with a telephone headset on. Several months had passed since his trip to New York, and he'd gotten his shot at Quicksolve. After a few months' wait, there was an opening and, with Jack's help, Michael worked his way into an entry-level technical support position.

Michael entered a support ticket into his computer when he heard a knock on the cubicle wall behind him. He turned and saw Jack smiling.

"What's going on?" Jack asked.

"Oh, the usual," Michael replied. "Doing support tickets. Funny how they come in waves."

Jack nodded, "Lots call during lunchtime trying to schedule that getaway trip. Any problem customers yet?"

Michael glanced back at his screen and said, "A few. Some people don't know a mouse from a cup of coffee."

"Yeah, takes a lot of patience, some of them."

"It's cool. No one's been a full blown ass yet. But hey, I had the roommate from hell not long ago, and I survived that." Michael laughed.

"Whatever happened to that guy? Brad, right?"

"Yep. Last I heard, he took a job offshore. Some two weeks on two weeks off deal."

"Nice."

"Guess it's better for him, he can be on time, and he doesn't have to be a prick on the mainland to people more than half the time."

"Ha! You're outta there anyway. Good riddance." Jack walked into Michael's cubicle to have a seat. "Hey, how about lunch? Just to catch up. You can tell me about the new apartment."

"Sounds good. Maybe 11:30?"

"You got it!"

They shook hands, and Jack left. Michael felt like he owed much to Jack. He continued with the support tickets until his phone rang. He saw his parents' phone number on the screen. He answered, "Good morning, Quicksolve, how may I be of assistance to you."

Michael's mother laughed on the other end. She said, "Oh stop now, you knew it was me. You're making me think I need to book a flight somewhere."

Michael chuckled, "Well, I'm here to help. How are you doing, Mom?"

"Oh I'm fine. Just getting over a sinus infection, but that's nothing too bad."

"Glad you're finally out of the hospital."

"Me too, baby. Had enough for a good while there."

"I bet."

"So how is my grandson?"

Michael swelled with pride. "Doing well, gonna be in little league with him this summer, and maybe we'll make a trip to the gulf coast."

"You still alright with that?"

"Yeah, it was a change for me, but I'm liking being part of this with Sarah."

"Mmmhm. Well just be careful, okay? You've got more mouths to feed now."

"I know-"

"-And I think it's great you taking on the other boy too. I know you like to do all you can."

"I'm fine, mom."

"Alright. Listen, your father and I are talking about taking a weekend trip to some vineyards on the Northshore near Covington."

"That sounds good."

"How is everything with your apartment?"

"Oh, it's fine, Mom. The landlord's decent, though he needs to get on this toilet issue. Been a month already. Other than that, going fine."

"Well hope that works out soon. If you ever need anything on that, just let us know, okay?"

"I know, Mom. Thanks."

"Sure, sweetheart. We love you!"

"Love you both too, Mom."

"I'll let you get back to work. Don't forget to visit soon."

"Oh I will, Mom. Thanks. Bye!"

"Bye sweetheart!"

Michael hung up the phone. He enjoyed the sense of independence he had with his own place, and he noticed a difference it made in the relationship with his parents. He felt almost as if they reached out to him more since he started supporting himself. The gap he'd felt between them for awhile was being closed, or at least it had a bridge laid across it now.

Michael finished up entering tickets when he saw an email in his inbox. He hadn't recognized the sender though the subject line got his attention: "Charlotte Ducrest auditions for new role." He opened the email and clicked on the link to an entertainment website for stories about Charlotte. He'd kept up with *Stewardesses* on Facebook, even though the series didn't make the cut and was canceled. The fan support was so strong that people remained on Facebook and even Twitter, periodically tweeted or checked in with each other, and maintained the friendships built through their shared following of the series.

The story about Charlotte went on to say that she was grateful for the opportunity *Stewardesses* gave her in the US entertainment market. Michael smiled at reading this. To him, it was almost like he watched a sibling, or even a significant other who'd gotten a big break in life and a chance at what they really wanted. He felt that finally, he also was close to what he wanted. He was working with technology, made good money, and he even considered some night classes in computers.

Michael clicked the comment link for the news story and entered: "Great news and best wishes to Charlotte, from one of your Louisiana fans!"

As he closed the website, he heard his phone's incoming text notification. He read the message, "Lunch plans?" He replied back, "Jack and I will be at the mall food court around 11:30. Want to join?" Another text soon followed: "Love to, see you there!"

Michael set his phone on his desk and searched for any additional outstanding support tickets. His office phone rang again. He answered to hear Greg, his supervisor's, voice.

"Michael, can you stop by my office right now?"

"On my way."

Michael grabbed his phone and walked out of his cubicle. He was afraid maybe Greg had gotten complaints from customers about him. Jack said it happened on occasion, but usually the customers were reasonable.

Michael stood at the open door of Greg's office. Greg was a short man, rotund with very little hair on his head. He was on the phone. He waved Michael in, and pointed at a chair in front of his desk.

Michael sat and glanced around Greg's office. A generic poster of islands hung on one wall, and a couple of plaques were on the wall behind where Greg sat.

Greg finished the call, and looked at Michael. "So, how're you doing?"

Michael said, "I'm fine, I guess. Everything alright?"

"Oh yeah, fine. Look, you've been here for a few months, and things are going well."

Michael sat up in his chair. He felt a slight wave of relief that the conversation leaned toward a commendation instead of a rebuke.

Greg continued, "As you know, we offer 24/7 support. It's time we work you into rotation."

Michael's mood dipped at the thought of night and weekend work. "What's involved?" He asked cautiously.

Greg replied, "Oh, you carry our phone for after hour calls. Typically you take a six-hour shift. You can take the hours off during the day during the week, kinda a comp time thing."

Michael nodded. "Okay, when does this start?"

Greg said, "Well, I can really use you this weekend. But I know I'm springing this on you last minute and all. How about you start next weekend?"

Michael's stomach tightened. He had plans with Sarah and her boys for then. They had been getting together frequently, but Michael also wanted to make sure he stepped up for his employer when needed. He realized the place he was in, and the job he had required more of a commitment from him. He knew this couldn't be handled like he did things in the past. He didn't want a repeat of Tech 4U. He said, "I need to make some arrangements, but that should work."

Greg smiled, "All right then. Christine at HR has the phone and what you'll need for this. Just go see her sometime after lunch, and she'll get you fixed up."

Michael nodded and said, "Is that all?"

"Sure. Catch the door when you leave?"

Michael got up from the chair as Greg picked up the phone again. Christine met him as he left Greg's office. She held a few papers in one hand. She adjusted her glasses and grinned. "So, you're our new 24/7 support crew member."

"Guess I am."

She smiled. "Here's a few forms to complete for your network access."

Michael grabbed the forms and looked them over. "Thanks, by the way."

"For what?"

"Your fiancé, the lawyer? He really saved Jack and me. We couldn't have made it through that lawsuit paying someone out of pocket."

She shrugged, "He told me it wasn't a huge issue. Lots of those things happening, apparently."

"Well it was huge for me and Jack."

"The least I could do for another *Stewardesses* fan." She winked.

"Of course." Michael smiled. "Owe you big!"

As he walked out into the cubicle area, he caught sight of Jack. Jack walked over to Michael and said, "Uh oh, coming outta the boss man's office? Everything okay?"

"Yeah," Michael sighed. "I'll be pulling after-hours support next weekend."

"I've been doing that for awhile. It's pretty easy."

"Great!"

"Unless of course the server blows up, and then you're screwed."

"Oh don't even mention that."

Jack chuckled. "It'll be fine."

"Yeah, it's just that I have... plans that weekend."

Jack said, "I see. It's part of the deal, I'm afraid."

Michael said, "Gotcha."

"Work's gotta come first sometimes."

"Besides, I've already ditched one job last year for plans."

Jack patted Michael on the back, "Good point, my friend. Look, don't worry about it. This comes up every few weeks. Just work around it. At least now you know, right?"

Michael said, "True. How about we hit the mall? I'm hungry!"

***

Michael and Jack sat at the food court in the Lakeside Shopping Center. They arrived slightly before 11:30, just before the lunch rush.

Between bites of his sandwich, Michael said, "By the way, company's joining us."

Jack took a sip of his drink and replied, "Company, huh? Is this who I think it is?"

Michael smiled. "Maybe. Hey man, I'll have the last of the money to you by next weekend."

Jack nodded, "I wasn't worried. I know where you live, and where you work!"

Michael laughed, "If it wasn't for you I wouldn't have money to pay you back."

"No worries. It's senior prom season, with June weddings just ahead!"

Michael laughed. "To think we were once just a lowly limo company."

"I'm impressed you got Kelly to come in on this party planning business with us."

Michael shrugged, "She was already coming back here for a month or two, plus how do you think I got her to make a detour from moving to drive Charlotte around?"

"Hah! Just when I thought you ditched your old ways," Jack chided.

"Ah, just think of it as closure on that part of my obsessions."

"Mmmhm," Jack said as he chuckled. "So Kelly just upped and forgot about culinary school?"

"Not all the way. She can pick it back up, but I guess trying something down here for a change got her excited."

Jack raised his cup, and toasted Michael's statement. Michael set down his sandwich and quickly touched his drink to Jack's. "Cheers, my friend."

As they set down their drinks, they heard a familiar voice. "Is this a private party, or can anyone join in?" There was Sarah with a tray of food court Chinese. Michael stood up from his seat, and kissed her on the lips. "Hey baby, how are you?"

Sarah smiled in return. "I'm really good." She set down her tray, and dug in. In between bites she asked, "So what are you two up to today?"

Michael said, "Oh, just saving the world for people trying to book vacations right away."

Sarah smirked, "Well I hope none of them are looking for our favorite stewardesses to handle that. Damn, I miss that show. I could have spent a few more weeks at least staring into John's eyes."

"At least Charlotte's still working."

"Still stalking her, bad boy?"

"Ehh a little," Michael shrugged.

Sarah beamed. Jack said, "Uh excuse me, you're not hanging on every breath, word and tweet from Charlotte Ducrest anymore?"

Michael nodded. Jack shook his head and asked, "Who are you, and what have you done with my friend Michael?"

"I've learned there are other things more worth my time," Michael said, returning Sarah's look.

The three of them laughed.

Michael took a sip of his drink. "Baby, about next weekend."

"Yes?" she replied.

"My boss just sprung this on me like ten minutes before we came here. They need me to handle weekend support for a few hours on Saturday. I know this screws up the plans we had, but wanted to tell you as soon as I knew."

Sarah chewed thoughtfully as she measured her response. "It's okay, really. The radio station is having a live broadcast, and I may just stop on by to chat with Vanessa and Peter."

"Ha, Peter. Has he gotten over how things went between you two yet?"

"Pretty much. He's a tough guy. Bullheaded and still an asshole, but at least now I know he has some underlying respect for me going on beneath all the strutting and crowing."

"At least the guy is consistent, right?"

"Yes, I suppose. Doesn't matter as much now that I'm not working for him anymore. I'm in accounting, so he's sending me reports now! He's my bitch for a change." Sarah smiled deviously.

"That's my girl. How are things there?"

"Oh not too bad. I'm so glad this promotion came along when it did. The pay is a bit better, the hours are decent, and I don't have to make after work events as much. Maybe there's a future for me there."

"That's great, though I miss seeing you working at Ales. You were the queen of pouring beer. Ever miss it?"

"Um, not so much. I'd rather have a steady income and nights free than work my little hiney to the bone. I miss being with the staff, but we're in there enough I can catch up with them when I want."

"This is true."

"I'm just glad Jimmy is back in jail. I swear. He graduates from meth to armed robbery?" Sarah shook her head. "It was bad enough he had to assault me."

211

Michael placed his hand atop hers. "Been a tough few months. But I'd take all that to be where we are."

Sarah nodded and offered a faint smile.

Michael asked her, "Sure you're okay with us changing plans? I mean, I don't have much choice, but I think you should have a say."

"It's fine, dear. I mean, sure I'd love to spend time with you, but it's one weekend. Really, it's just one day, and not even a whole day. Tell me though, is this going to be a regular thing?"

Jack chimed in, "They give us this shift every few weeks."

Michael glanced at Jack, then back at Sarah. Sarah took a sip of her drink, and then said, "We'll be fine."

Michael reached to touch Sarah's shoulder. She smiled back at him. Sarah asked Jack, "How are things with you?"

"Oh good days, bad days," Jack replied. "Dunno where things are gonna end up with Ashlyn. Still speak to her a few times a month."

Sarah nodded.

As Michael sipped the rest of his drink, Sarah and Jack finished their food. He slowly leaned back in his chair, and watched people as they milled around them in the food court. He realized that he looked at people a little differently than he had when he worked at B&G. Instead of feeling like he observed people in the midst of lives much more interesting than his own, he now felt a little more productive, and like his life was on par with the busy people who moved about where they sat, many of them probably on lunch breaks from their own jobs. He felt like he had some direction. He and Sarah were doing well together. He also felt good about his job and prospects.

Michael shook his cup, then set it back down and said, "We should get together again soon, when we're not in a hurry to get back to work. Why don't we go to the Lakefront, like this weekend? I've been trying to go there for awhile, well damn it let's just do it. What do you think?"

Sarah and Jack glanced at Michael as he spoke. Sarah smiled and grabbed Michael's arm. "Sounds great, baby. We can see the Mardi Gras Fountain, the boys like that. And I know they'd be up for tossing a ball around or something. Little league hasn't started just yet, so we do have some time."

Michael smiled at Sarah. He turned to Jack. "What do you think, man? We can pack a few beers, maybe have a picnic lunch out there. You can give me a hand with the kids."

Jack looked at Michael. He glanced off, as if he checked an invisible calendar next to Michael's head. "I'm in, what time?"

Michael looked back at Sarah. "What do you think? Between the two of us I think we can get Taylor and Alex in gear by 9. Maybe, 10 out by the picnic area? That should give us enough time to have some fun before we eat."

Sarah glanced back at Michael. "Look at you being the daddy and planning things out. This mama says let's see how it goes. I think that's a good time to shoot for. Jack, if we're late, just call us. Odds are we'll be on our way."

Jack nodded, "Not a problem. See y'all then!"

Chapter Twenty-nine

When Michael, Sarah and her boys arrived at the Lakefront, they found many other people had a similar idea that day. It wasn't too big a surprise, being a Saturday morning in April when even people in school were ready for any break until summer hit. The air was warm, with a slight breeze off of Lake Pontchartrain. The sky was mostly clear, except for a few small clouds. The sun shone down brilliantly. It was a perfect New Orleans day, bright and sunny but not too hot just yet.

Michael drove Sarah's car along with the rest in a medium slow procession down the twisting Lakeshore Drive. The road was blocked off to only allow traffic to flow one way. Each vehicle was filled with people who glanced out of the windows. Some leaned out and shouted a greeting to friends nearby.

As they looked at the crowds in cars and on foot, Sarah asked, "Where do you think we should park? Getting pretty crowded here."

"I'm going to try the picnic area. And if not, I know some other spots up ahead," Michael replied. "Jack better not wait too long, or he'll be walking a ways to get to us."

Sarah nodded at Michael and glanced back to Taylor and Alex. They were engrossed in some game on their iPod touch and were silent at the moment. She tapped Taylor on the knee. "Guys, we're almost here. Ready to have some fun?"

Alex glanced up at Sarah's voice and looked out his window. Taylor replied, "What're we doing first?"

Sarah replied, "Well, we need to find a picnic spot. And then why don't you three toss the football around?"

Michael glanced up briefly in the rear view mirror. "We'll play Saints football. I'll be Drew Brees, and y'all can be Mark Ingram and Marques Colston."

Alex turned to look at Michael in the rear view mirror and Taylor said, "Woo!"

Michael found a spot near the picnic area of the lake. The parking spots were off Lakeshore Drive nearby a traffic circle, and immediately in front of a spot in the levee where a set of concrete steps and railing were available for access. Several other cars were parked nearby. As Michael parked, he pulled his phone out. Sarah exited the car, and she made sure Taylor and Alex helped carry a few supplies.

Michael called his voicemail and heard a message from Jack:

"Hey man, I can't make it. I'm still feeling kinda weird about the whole situation with Ashlyn, and actually she called me the other day to scream at me about something I signed us up for awhile back, and... well, I'm rambling now. It's just a little rough at the moment, I don't think I'll be very good company today. Call you guys later."

Michael gritted his teeth. He felt bad about Jack's issue with Ashlyn. He looked at Sarah and the boys loaded up with items. "Coming, baby?" she asked.

Michael put his phone back on his belt holster and walked up to Sarah. She saw the change in his expression. "What's wrong? You didn't get a call from work did you?"

"Jack's not coming."

"Why not?"

"Ashlyn called him up, and they got into it. Guess the guy's still adjusting a little bit. He sounded pretty down."

"I never was quite sure about her. Seemed a little too, I don't

215

know... uppity for my taste. Like one of these uptown chicks or something, always bragging about their clothes, or what parties they're going to."

Alex held a bag of potato chips and a football. He interrupted Sarah and Michael to say, "Mommy, we still going to the lake?"

Sarah replied, "Yes baby. We're waiting to see if Mr. Jack is coming." She looked back to Michael. "Well, we're here. I made a lunch. We're having this picnic if he comes or not." She walked again towards the stairs over the levee, as Alex and Taylor followed suit. Michael looked around and spied the ice chest he had packed, on the ground near their car. He grabbed it and caught up as they made their way over the steps.

When they reached the other side of the levee they were greeted with a wooded picnic area. Several pavilions, each with a picnic table were littered about the area. Numerous trees provided an ample amount of shade. While the air was still warm, they wouldn't have much concern with direct sunlight here. The lake stretched out in the distance, the shimmering water invited them closer.

Of the pavilions, four were already occupied. They went to a vacant one not far from the edge of the picnic area by the lake. Sarah set down containers of cold cuts, bread and a small ice chest packed with potato salad. The boys followed up behind her.

Michael surveyed the area and said, "Sweet, I think we are ready now. Lemme see if I can change Jack's mind about not coming."

Michael pulled out his phone again and walked off a few feet from the pavilion. He looked at the lake as he called Jack's number. The sound in his voice matched the mood on his voicemail. "Hello?"

"Dude, I got your message. You okay?"

"Bad time. Can't we do this later? Just gonna watch some movies, and maybe grab a beer."

Michael paused. He'd been down before, and certainly related to Jack on the whole relationship gone wrong thing, but still he wanted Jack brought out of his current mood. After all, Jack and Sarah had done the same for him. "You know, Sarah put a lot into this, thinking we'd all come out, and have a little fun. We've been trying to do this for awhile, just slow down the busy schedules, and have a good time, you know?"

"You and her and the kids are there, why not just let this be for y'all? We'll try later."

Michael glanced back toward the pavilion where Sarah and the boys were. She took the football and lightly tossed it to Taylor and Alex. Michael said, "Look, you mentioned Ashlyn, and that whole situation with her is still bugging you out. It isn't going to change much today. Just come on out, and drink a few beers with us, man. Remember when I was all down about myself, and I felt like I was going nowhere? Well, a good friend of mine told me I shouldn't just wait for things to happen."

Jack laughed a bit on the phone. "Um, yeah."

"Come on, man, work with me. Point I'm trying to get at, I'm here for you. Sarah's here for you. I know you're in an awkward place, but you need to get outta that funk for a little while. Come on out, have a beer. I bet you'll feel better."

There was a pause on the other end. Michael asked, "You still there? I wasn't that long winded, was I?"

Jack sighed, "Alright dude. Gimme a few minutes. Where y'all parked?"

"Picnic area near the traffic circle."

Jack arrived in the picnic area about half an hour later. Dressed in a t-shirt and shorts with tennis shoes, he slowly walked by the other pavilions, until he spotted them. Michael and the boys were into a game of catch, the three of them stood several yards apart from each other, in a triangular pattern. Sarah was under the pavilion, she sipped an Abita Amber and watched them. She caught sight of Jack and waved.

As Jack walked closer to the pavilion, Michael noticed him. He called out, "Yo, Jackster! Let's see what ya got!" With that, Michael hurled the football in Jack's direction. The pass was a bit high, but Jack leaped up anyway. He tipped the ball slightly as it sailed overhead.

"Aww, weak, man! You can do better than that!"

"Hey, throw it in my zip code next time."

They both laughed. Jack trotted back to where the ball landed, picked it up and tossed it back in Michael's direction. He headed to the pavilion. As he neared, Sarah reaching her arms out for an embrace.

As they hugged, she said, "Tough time, dear?"

"Sucks having drama."

They released their embrace. Sarah smiled at him, "Glad you're here. I have enough assholes in my life already, I need to up my quotient of friends."

"Friends are good. Think I need to let things go for a bit with Ashlyn. I was trying to make things more civil and that bombed."

"Sometimes you need to let the past simmer. Want a beer?"

"Yeah, that's great. What do you have?"

"Plenty of Abita. Amber, Turbodog, Purple Haze?"

"Turbodog is fine."

Sarah popped open the beer and handed it to Jack. Sarah and Jack sat down at the table on opposite sides.

"So where's Kelly?" Jack asked.

"She said something about picking up supplies from Restaurant Depot. Girl can't stand still whether she's here or in New York." Sarah marveled.

"Well that's good," Jack replied. "We need our catering manager to be on top of things!"

Sarah laughed, "I still can't believe it took Charlotte Ducrest to snap Michael out of that funk. Kelly told me about their little deal."

"Yeah, I gotta say, I didn't even see that coming. Guess there was more going on in Michael's head other than TV shows and actresses after all." Jack winked.

Sarah's eyebrow arched. Michael joined them back at the table as Taylor and Alex played on by themselves.

Sarah asked Michael, "So, still sure you're done with Charlotte?"

Reaching for a beer, Michael quipped, "Ya know, I thought about it. They wore those girdles in that outfit, right? Too much to negotiate. Deal breaker for me." Sarah tossed a balled up napkin at him.

Jack asked Sarah, "How's Kelly's seizure thing?"

Michael added, "Yeah, she doesn't say much that isn't about work."

Sarah studied her beer bottle. "She's been without incident for a few months. The doctors have her on a few prescriptions, but as long as she takes them she should be fine. I'm relieved, y'all. She has that drive to be successful as a chef. When she had to leave, and it looked like it wouldn't happen for her, I could see the disappointment in her eyes."

Michael nodded. "Right, yeah. I can sure relate. I'm still looking for that business idea of my own. Of course, may finally be on to something now."

"I think you are. And hey Jack, as an ex-girlfriend of yours who still cares a lot about you, I suggest you let it rest with Ashlyn. I know you're down, and that's fine, I've been there. But get your mind off her as much as you can. It didn't work, that happens. At least you don't have a marriage, or kids to add to the attachments. Clean breaks are always best."

Jack nodded. They heard some yelling and turned to see Taylor doing what appeared to be some kind of "touchdown dance". Alex tried to strip the ball from Taylor, and they both fell to the ground. As they started roughhousing, Michael trotted up and reached down to pull them apart. Sarah set down her beer, but then Michael had them sufficiently calmed down. *Way to go, Michael,* she thought. *Maybe I finally have a true partner here.*

"He seems to have taken well to being a dad." Jack remarked.

"Yeah, he really has. Hard to believe that's the same man who at one point couldn't stop ogling a TV actress long enough to hold a conversation."

They both laughed. Jack turned back to Sarah and said, "I like how we have something now that looks to be really good for us. And Kelly being involved, I think we may have hit onto something big."

Michael and the boys headed back under the pavilion. When they were near the table, Michael stooped to set the football near one of the posts of the pavilion. He then sat down next to Sarah. He reached into the ice chest near the table, grabbed an Abita Turbodog and opened it. Slightly winded, he took a sip of beer and turned to Jack. "Now that was a workout. You've gotta help me out on the next one, man, these guys have boundless energy."

Jack nodded and raised his bottle of beer. "I'll do what I can."

Sarah got up from the table and fixed some food for Taylor and Alex. The boys had sat on the far end and munched on sandwiches, potato chips and drank Cokes.

Michael and Jack glanced at Sarah as she set up food for the boys. Michael then turned to Jack, saying, "I'm glad you came out today, man. I know it's not easy, but making the effort is good." They clinked their bottles together as if to toast on Michael's sentiment.

Sarah returned back to her seat next to Michael and grabbed her bottle of beer. "What a great day. And having those two over there playing nice is no small miracle, let me tell you." She nodded in the direction of Taylor and Alex.

Michael said, "We're only at halftime. Gotta run this energy out of them so they don't keep climbing the walls at night, right?"

"Yep. At least now I've got help when they're stir crazy at home." She leaned into Michael, bumping shoulders with him.

"I'd like to say something," Michael said.

Sarah and Jack looked at Michael. Michael placed his hands on the table, looked down and then back at them. "I just want to thank you both. You're two of the people I'm closest with, and your support and friendship has meant the world to me."

Sarah chimed in, "Well, it's fair to say you and I are a lot more than friends now."

Michael smiled and kissed Sarah on the lips. "Yes, that is true."

Jack waved his hands about in mock disgust. "Get a room you two, I'm trying to drink here!"

"Hey, I saw enough PDA from you in the past, buddy. Cut me some slack here," Michael laughed.

Jack smiled at Michael. Sarah reached out to touch Michael's hand. Michael continued, "I know I haven't always made the best choices. But knowing that the two of you have been there, and will continue to be there, means so much to me. Maybe I won't make all the right choices in the future. But I know I'll be able to count on you when I need help, and please know that you can count on me."

Jack nodded and so did Sarah.

Jack added, "Thanks for getting me out here. Just getting my

220

mind off things is helping."

Michael nodded and smiled. "No one makes it alone, man." He raised his bottle. "To us."

Sarah and Jack raised their bottles to Michael and replied, "To us."

Michael smiled at them. Jack said, "Did I miss the food part of this picnic? Where's Sarah's down home cooking?"

Sarah remarked, "No, we were just getting warmed up, and there's plenty of sandwiches to go around. I don't know how much I would call it 'down home cooking', but it's the finest any local grocery store in New Orleans can provide, tell you that much!"

Michael said, "Then out with it. I'm starving!"

Excerpt

On the following pages, we've included an excerpt from "The Harvest", a short story by Paul Heingarten, available exclusively for Amazon Kindle and all devices running the Amazon Kindle App.

PAUL HEINGARTEN

THE HARVEST

A SHORT STORY

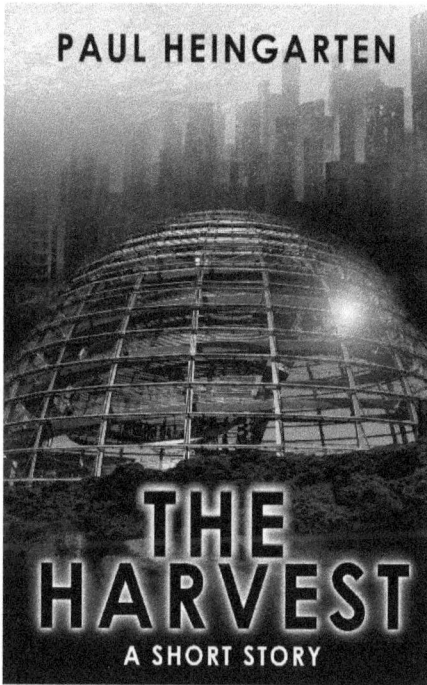

Kyle, 17, wants to believe what he's been taught all his life: he and the chosen kids in his colony have been training to work the Harvest, producing the only food the world will soon have. But another colony kid, Devora, has learned just what the Harvest is, and is hell bent on saving Kyle and the other kids from lies they've all been fed.

Devora isn't new to being a spectacle. A castoff with no parents, she's no stranger to colony punishments. Even Allie, Devora's bunk mate, would be in much worse shape if not for Kyle's help with instruction classes and physical training. Allie joins Devora's cause and tries to enlist Kyle.

Devora and Allie… two troublemakers. Or are they?

As Kyle nears graduation, things begin to unravel as Devora disappears from the colony. Then, his bunk mate vanishes, only to return badly beaten. Desperate for answers, he receives only calculated direction from Anton, the colony proctor as well as the staff of instructors and protectors intent on maintaining discipline at all costs.

Does Kyle trust what he's been taught all along? Or does he take the word of Devora and Allie about the real problem they face?

THE HARVEST
by Paul Heingarten

I'm lucky.

That's what my instructors have been telling me, telling all of us. We're lucky. The chosen ones. Born into a life where we'll serve and make this world a better one.

My name is Kyle. I'm part of colony Gamma, a facility within the country of Ordine on earth. I'm here along with about two thousand other kids. There's kids from my age, seventeen, all the way down to newborns. No parents though. We're here because we're training for the Harvest.

I'm lying in my bunk. I can tell it's almost time to start the day as I hear Randal shifting about on the bunk above me.

"Sleep good?" I ask.

He retorts with random mumbling.

"Come on, full day of training ahead."

Then he manages speech. "Yeah, up and at 'em."

Our dormitory room has enough space for two people. As Randal stands before the grooming console I grab my uniform and tools for the day. Picks, digital monitors, environment processor.

"Can't believe we're almost finished here," Randal says.

I catch his glimpse in the mirror. "I know. Two more weeks and then Harvest."

"How do you think it'll be?"

"Tough, but you know what they said, if we don't finish this, everything's gone."

What we've been taught, since we're five and able to attend school in the colony, is that Earth underwent a massive blight due to a bad meteor shower thirty years ago. The air got so bad on the surface that the population began living underground in large caverns. Livestock were wiped out and most crops weren't sustainable. One crop, a bean called mendacium, managed to survive so fields of it were planted. They hoped one day it would be enough to feed the world. But that kind of yield takes time, so all available food was rationed while they worked on building the mendacium crop and a group big enough to work it.

The earliest Harvest workers died from working in the thick

dust clouds the meteorites left behind. The mendacium they could supply was small, but each year brought a little more from the yield. Our smarter minds figured out the tools and gear needed. Everyone developed a system for raising hands to get the job done. That's us, the colony kids.

Ready for the day, we join our classmates walking the pathways to the Instruction Facility. A sea of plain blue uniforms flows toward a towering gray building in the center of the colony, where all our training takes place. It's also the admin building. The ceiling of the colony dome displays an artificial sky of blue with swirling clouds.

Scattered along our way are the Protectors, a kind of security for us. The entrances to the colony are heavily guarded, since we have all the food and shelter that many on the outside would kill to get. The Protectors keep us safe. To look at one you wouldn't want to cross them anyway. Their big hulking armor suits and pulse rifles are enough for me to keep in line for sure.

As we walk I hear someone call, "Kyle?"

Glancing to the right I see Anton, Proctor of the Colony standing on the side of the path and motioning to me. I tell Randal I'll catch up and slip over to see Anton. His dark gray uniform is always pristine and his jet black hair never out of place.

"Yes sir?"

"After morning class, you have a holovisit."

"Okay."

"Stop by the comm center, it'll be waiting." His smile doesn't break his stern gaze. The government put proctors like Anton in total charge of their assigned colonies. It's his task to get us ready for Harvest. I heard rumors about how he handled anyone who caused trouble around the colony. I've seen bruises on some of my classmates and heard enough of their stories to be careful around him.

As I join the group again, I feel a small sting on the back of my head.

"Hi goober."

Allie.

Turning my head I say, "Hey."

"Wanna know something?"

"From you? Doubt it."

Another flick.

"Hey! Cut that out."

She walks closer to whisper in my ear, "Devora tried to get out last night."

"Why?"

"She saw something. Something she wasn't supposed to."

"Devora's a loudmouth with a big imagination," I scoff. Devora. She's maybe two or three years younger than me. Always questioning in class, always being held back and disciplined.

"It's real, Kyle. Meet me after morning session."

"Can't, I have a holovisit."

"Well then afternoon."

"Maybe."

She sighs. "Come on, it's important."

Allie can be such a pain. There are some kids who just can't follow along at times. But I try and help Allie out when I can. She owes me for helping her out with the fitness requirements here, that's for sure. Just don't need her roping me into anything bad.

End of Excerpt

About the Author

Paul Heingarten spreads time between writing, being a musician, and, since 2002, a career in Information Technology. His articles for websites like EzineArticles.com, and fan fiction pieces for FanFiction.net (pseudonym WistfulGuy), have been accessed and downloaded thousands of times. He lives in the southern United States with his wife Andrea.

One more thing...

I hope you enjoyed reading this story. I'm working on many more and would love to keep in touch with you to let you know when I have more available. Please go to www.paulheingarten.com and click on the Email List link to sign up for my spam free email list.

www.ingramcontent.com/pod-product-compliance
Lightning Source LLC
Chambersburg PA
CBHW021924040426
42448CB00008B/906